"Rev. Jesse Lee Peterson is a great American. He is a man of conscience with a bold prescription to make America a better place."

—SEAN HANNITY

"*Scam* is a devastating analysis and critique of how black politicians and the civil-rights establishment have delivered one disaster after another for black Americans. Indeed, it's an account of what's nothing less than a gross betrayal of those who gave their blood, sweat and tears to make today's liberty and opportunities possible. Rev. Peterson's solutions are just the simple common-sense of our ancestors, something all too rare today."

—WALTER E. WILLIAMS, *Professor of Economics, George Mason University*

"Rev. Jesse Lee Peterson has become one of the more principled black conservative moral leaders in our country. His tenacity and leadership is a throwback to the leadership of Booker T. Washington. Black America, *all of America*, needs more leaders like Rev. Peterson."

—NIGER INNIS, *the national spokesperson for C.O.R.E. (Congress of Racial Equality)*

"Bucking the racial stereotype is hard work. I know because I've been doing it for years. Allies in the fight to promote racial good health are difficult to find. The Rev. Jesse Peterson has what it takes to point America toward better race relations."

—KEN HAMBLIN, *"The Black Avenger"*

"Jesse Peterson exemplifies two qualities rare in any age, and certainly rare in our own: a passion for truth and extraordinary courage."

—DENNIS PRAGER

"I give the Reverend Peterson high marks for his unrelenting willingness to expose those media anointed and self-appointed black leaders who've made a long and lucrative career posing as the mouthpiece of blacks. Despite my deep disagreement with the Rev. Peterson on many issues, I salute him for having the courage to challenge the black establishment and for always remaining true to his beliefs."

—DR. EARL OFARI HUTCHINSON, *nationally syndicated columnist, author of* The Crisis in Black and Black

SCAM

REV. JESSE LEE PETERSON

SCAM

HOW *the* BLACK LEADERSHIP
EXPLOITS BLACK AMERICA

WND BOOKS

Nashville
www.WNDBooks.com

Published in Nashville, Tennessee, by WND Books.

GRANDPA (TELL ME 'BOUT THE GOOD OLD DAYS)
© 1985 Sony/ATV Tunes LLC
All rights adm. by Sony/ATV Music Publishing, 8 Music Sq. W., Nashville, TN 37203.
All Rights Reserved. Used By Permission.

Library of Congress Cataloging-in-Publication Data

Peterson, Jesse Lee, 1949-
    Scam : how the Black leadership exploits Black America / Jesse Lee Peterson.
    p. cm.
    1. African American leadership. 2. African Americans—Social conditions—
1975- 3. African Americans—Politics and government. 4. African American
politicians—Biography. 5. United States—Race relations. 6. Racism—United
States. I. Title.
E185.615.P438 2003
305.896'073—dc22   2003014466

Printed in the United States of America

03 04 05 06 07 — 5 4 3 2 1

To Justice Clarence Thomas:
you are the example of what black
Americans should be.

CONTENTS

Introduction

—ɯ—

B lack Americans have been scammed; what's worse, they've been scammed by their own folks. What you are about to read in this book is the truth about who the scammers are, how they've conned black America, and what can be done about it.

Over a decade ago, I began to realize that the so-called black leaders like Jesse Jackson, Louis Farrakhan, Al Sharpton, and others were lying about why blacks are in trouble today. If some blacks wonder why things don't improve despite this "leadership," they need to wake up to the fact that these leaders profit by creating hatred and animosity between the races. In fact, it is imperative for these leaders to continue creating problems even where none exist. If they don't, they're out of business. And they're definitely not that—their business is flush. They've been running a scam on black Americans since Dr. Martin

Luther King Jr. died that fateful morning in Memphis. Dr. King did indeed have a dream, but Jesse Jackson has turned it into a nightmare.

Former slave Booker T. Washington, author of *Up from Slavery*, is one of my heroes. He was dealing with his own version of Jesse Jackson back in the late 19th and early 20th centuries. He warned about "problem profiteers" who make their living by causing racial strife:

> There is a class of colored people who make a business of keeping the troubles, the wrongs, and the hardships of the Negro race before the public. Having learned that they are able to make a living out of their troubles, they have grown into the settled habit of advertising their wrongs—partly because they want sympathy and partly because it pays. Some of these people do not want the Negro to lose his grievances, because they do not want to lose their jobs.[1]

Sound familiar?

These "leaders" have been brainwashing blacks since Washington's day, blaming white Americans for all of our problems. Sometimes these problems are created, sometimes just exacerbated, but always paraded to create racial hatred against whites. The big problem here: if a person can get you to hate, this person can control you! You never shake the genuine problems and you get shackled to suffocating resentments. I became a free man for the first time in my life by giving up hatred. If other blacks could understand this, they'd be free, too.

REVEALING THE LIE

I was raised on a cotton plantation near Montgomery and Tuskegee, Alabama, in the late '40s and early '50s and worked side by side with my grandparents in the sweltering heat, picking cotton. I would start to work early in the morning, take time off in the afternoon, and then continue picking cotton until the sun went down. When it was harvest time, I missed school in order to work. Despite having to endure backbreaking work in the fields, no one in my family blamed the "white man" for our plight. In fact, I don't recall anyone in my family expressing anger at whites for our economic condition. We knew that we had to make a living, and we were grateful for having jobs, regardless of how difficult it may have been for us.

I grew up in Alabama at a time when public schools were still segregated, when blacks were refused service in restaurants and had to use different restrooms. I understand the evils of segregation and believe it was important for black leaders like Dr. Martin Luther King Jr. to fight for the abolition of this social evil. But today, as I look back on my life and the condition of the black family during those times, I am convinced that by many different measures blacks were actually better off then than they are now—after forty years of the civil rights movement and the agitations of so-called black leaders like Jesse Jackson.

Back then, by and large, we had good black schools, fine black universities, safe and well-groomed black communities, and intact families. Today, by most measures, the black family is in a shambles: black communities are drug-infested, single parenthood is the norm, and crime is rampant in the black areas of our major cities.

In a way, my life was a preview of much to come for many black Americans. I was born into a broken family in the tiny town of Comer Hill, Alabama. I did not know my father, and my mother had left me with her mother when I was a toddler and moved to Gary, Indiana, with another man.

I first met my father when I was about thirteen. One day he just showed up at my grandmother's house in Comer Hill. When he told me who he was, I was incredibly excited he had come to see me. As I studied him, I felt completed, like a missing piece of my life had been supplied to me. I immediately felt the natural awareness that a father is critically important to a child and that a boy needs his father to help him grow into a man. He told me to come visit him in Indiana where he lived. Since I sometimes spent summers with my mother, who also lived in Indiana then, I did get out to see him but had to do it behind her back. For reasons I didn't understand at the time, she hated my father and tried to prevent me from seeing him. During those summers I began to understand why my mother and stepfather had always been so cold to me: I looked too much like him. That likeness—along with her anger for my father—caused her to reject me. My stepfather tried hard to be kind and loving toward me, but I wanted my father, and stepfather was no substitute. To both my stepfather and my mother, I represented an unpleasant memory.

When I was eighteen years old, I left Alabama and moved to Los Angeles to start a new life, having no idea what my future would hold for me. Unfortunately, I began listening to the teachings of men like Jesse Jackson, NAACP leaders, and Nation of Islam leader Louis Farrakhan. As a result of listening to these scam artists, I developed a hatred of the white man for what were actually my own personal failings, and I became even more confused about my own purpose for living. I began to use drugs as a way of coping with my inner turmoil. I also learned to think of welfare as an entitlement that America owed me for years of slavery and segregation.

In fact, I found it amazingly easy to get on welfare and simply live off the system. I signed up in Los Angeles and started receiving $300 a month. In addition, the system paid my rent and supplied me with food stamps, free medical coverage, and other benefits. I was making the white man pay me back for all of the oppression I thought I'd been subjected to in the past. So I partied with that money, caroused with women, and lived a fairly degenerate life. I thought I had it made.

But while on welfare, things didn't get better. They got worse. The more money I got from welfare, the less desire I had to work. It became spiritually and morally suffocating.

Looking for answers, I started to realize that I was being held back in life because of my own anger. It wasn't the white man who was oppressing me; it was my own anger, resentment, and hatred. It wasn't white racism keeping me on welfare; it was actually my own racism that was keeping me enslaved to a system as evil as slavery was before the Civil War. I also began to realize that much of what passes for religion or Christianity today in black churches is nothing more than the corrupt leadership of men. They rarely preach the truth about God; instead, they preach race hatred, vain philosophies, and liberal politics.

Once I uncovered the lie, I broke out of the shackles, and I've been trying to help others break free ever since.

SPREADING THE TRUTH

My message to the black man and to the black community is one of hope and encouragement, not one of anger and despair. I firmly believe that we blacks are our own worst enemies. By listening to the "problem profiteers" and blaming white America for our difficulties, we're handicapping ourselves and living unproductive and self-destructive lives. It is time to stop the excuse-mongering, claiming that whites are crippling our ability to get ahead. If blacks do not abandon this mentality and this rage against white America—if we do not accept responsibility for our own failures—we will forever remain defeated.

America is the land of opportunity; it gives blacks a greater chance for social and economic advancement than anywhere else in the world. Blacks should adopt the ideals of success, hard work, saving money, sustained effort, and self-restraint. They must maintain their mental health by adopting love as the controlling attitude in their lives rather than resentment and rage. In America, individuals control their own destinies. Those who want to succeed will do so, while those who choose to pity themselves and blame others will continue to fail.

With our current crop of black leaders in positions of power, it is unlikely that the plight of blacks will improve any time soon. I prefer to heed the wise words of Booker T. Washington: "I would permit no man to drag down my soul by making me hate him."[2] I'd take Booker T. Washington's advice over any current black leader who has a financial and political interest in creating and sustaining racial hatred in this nation.

It is time someone stood up to Jesse Jackson and organizations such as the NAACP, to world-class racist Louis Farrakhan, and to Al Sharpton, Maxine Waters, and many of America's black preachers, who are fleecing the flock instead of leading them to spiritual and physical freedom.

Saying such things isn't popular. Believe me, I know. I get called "nigger" quite a bit—and "Uncle Tom" and "sellout"—usually by fellow blacks. I've had guns drawn on me, my privacy and property grievously threatened—you name it. Do I enjoy that? No, I don't. But do you know something? My life is an absolute blessing, and I wouldn't trade it for anything.

Among many other things, I am known as the man who started the National Day of Repudiation of Jesse Jackson, which my organization, BOND (Brotherhood Organization of a New Destiny), hosts every year. We're also actively boycotting the NAACP. At BOND we're rebuilding the family by rebuilding the man: building character in this and the next generation of men (and women), while boldly standing for truth in the public square. With all the racial hustlers and agitators who pit people against each other for profit and status, there's an incredible amount of cleanup to do. But at BOND we're taking care of business.

These leaders need to be unseated, removed, boycotted, bounced, dismissed, junked, and jettisoned. Black Americans don't need leaders. We need individual responsibility, love of God and neighbor, the freedom to succeed or fail, and a life unshackled by hatred or resentment.

That's what this book is about: freeing blacks from the stranglehold of our so-called leaders and their poisoned words and deeds so we can stake out our true position in this land and recapture the stolen dream of Dr. King.

1

Blacks Need No Leaders

—ɯ—

*The day of the leader must end—
the dawn of the individual must arise*

Black Americans do not need the kind of self-appointed leaders they currently have. I don't recall the entire black race in this country taking a national vote to elect Jesse Jackson, Al Sharpton, Louis Farrakhan, the NAACP, California Congresswoman Maxine Waters, the Congressional Black Caucus, or liberal black preachers as our leaders, yet they've seized the mantle of leadership and claim to speak for all blacks in this nation.

Their leadership, however, has proven to be disastrous. These arrogant elitists have given us a continuous diet of racism, paranoia, affirmative action programs, and higher welfare checks; and many display little or no personal integrity in their own lives.

These self-proclaimed leaders have helped grow a welfare system that has resulted in the elimination of the black man as head of the family and placed the government as the "daddy" in most black families today. As a result, the civil rights leaders have become the head of the people.

Nearly 70 percent of all black children are born out of wedlock.[1] The welfare system was originally set up to pay recipients more money for each child, so this provided incentives for welfare moms to have more children rather than to care for those they already have. (The Welfare Reform Act passed in 1996 has helped encourage moms to get off of welfare, but this process is far from over.)

Current black leaders preach racial hatred and welfare dependency, not peace and independence. They earn their fat salaries by stirring up the racial pot and portraying blacks as the hopeless victims of racism. Unfortunately, most blacks have accepted these men and women as their new slave masters and have allowed these individuals to speak for them. We don't need their leadership.

It is a dangerous thing for a person to blindly put himself under the leadership of any man or woman. Blacks who allow themselves to be led around like sheep by the likes of Jesse Jackson are forfeiting their independence and free will. These leaders almost inevitably exploit their followers. These current black leaders tell blacks how to think, whom to vote for, and how to live their lives.

By preaching race hatred and the cleverly packaged ideology of socialism, these leaders have convinced millions of blacks that white America owes them special treatment: welfare checks, affirmative action programs, and even different grading systems in our nation's universities. Black educators have even created a fictional *Afrocentrist* history that pushes phony notions of black racial superiority in our nation's schools. Other educators have devised what they call *critical race theory,* which claims that there's no such thing as objective reality—that "rationality" is simply a tool of white males and is designed to oppress minorities.

Black preachers who have been seduced by these deadly attitudes and political philosophies are perpetuating a cycle of hatred and violence within the black community. They, too, have given up any reason or logic in their preaching and simply parrot the latest politically correct opinions from the Jacksons and Sharptons.

These pastors maintain control of their congregations by instilling a sense of fear in them. Black churchgoers are told that if they challenge the preacher, they're sinning against God. This fear-based manipulation keeps black churchgoers under the domination of these preachers who line their pockets with the tithes of their cult-like followers.

I frequently have black preachers on my daily radio program and have debated them in public forums and on TV. I have seen firsthand how they react when their ideas are challenged. They typically resort to name-calling, accusing me of being condemnatory and judgmental, and incorrectly citing Scripture to chastise me. Every now and then, they even accuse me of being an "Uncle Tom" or a "house nigger"—anything to dodge dealing with facts.

Several years ago, I interviewed the Rev. Leonard Jackson, a pastor at the First African Methodist Episcopal Church (FAME) in Los Angeles. I challenged Jackson to explain why his church and its senior pastor Cecil Murray were handing out "AIDS Prevention" packets to church members when these packets contained condoms. I was astonished by his reply. He denied that his church was telling its members, in essence, "Here's a condom—go out and have sex out of wedlock." But then he justified the condom distribution program by saying that AIDS is a major health problem and there are people who will choose to have sex outside of marriage.

By passing out condoms to his flock, Rev. Murray and his staff members are sinning against their congregation and their surrounding community. They should be preaching abstinence—not giving mixed messages to their churchgoers about sexuality and immoral behavior. When you hand a condom to a church member, you're saying it's okay to engage in unsafe sexual behaviors outside of marriage.

This lax attitude about sex should come as no surprise. Rev. Murray's church is a Hollywood celebrity church. In addition, Murray is a long-time supporter of Bill Clinton and Jesse Jackson.

When it was discovered that Jesse Jackson had fathered an illegitimate child with his secret mistress, Cecil Murray responded with these words: "His enemies will have a weapon, but his friends will have an opportunity, and that is to show forgiveness." He told ABC News that when his congregation learned of Jackson's outrageous behavior, it was met with a "shrug of the shoulders." "It is not that you discount it, it is not that you have no moral assessment, and that you have no concern," said Murray. "But he has said he made a mistake. He is taking care of the child."[2]

Of course, Murray's support for Jackson—despite Jackson's immoral conduct—isn't really a surprise because Jackson's Los Angeles Rainbow-PUSH organization maintains an office inside Cecil Murray's Renaissance Corporation Building!*

Today, the black church isn't a place where one goes to overcome sin. It's a place where one can go and deny the very existence of sin. Sexual and political sins are winked at by these liberal pastors, while they seem to spend all of their waking hours creating racist attitudes in their congregations.

CORRUPTION AT THE HIGHEST LEVELS

The corruption of the black church starts at the top and trickles down into the congregations. Churchgoers eventually become just like their leaders, and sin flourishes without any sense of accountability. Several years ago, Baptist leader Rev. Henry Lyons was arrested and eventually went to jail for embezzlement and fraud. Lyons headed up the National Baptist Convention, a black organization that claimed at the time to represent the interests of five to eight million black church members.

As it turned out, this figure was a myth perpetuated by Lyons to make the NBC look like it had more influence than it did. According to Bonita Henderson, a former aide to Lyons, he created an inflated membership list so he could sell the mailing lists to corporations for marketing purposes. Henderson says the NBC has fewer than seven thousand churches and its mailing list has never been larger than fifteen thousand members.[3]

---

*BOND held its 4th annual National Day of Repudiation of Jesse Jackson Rally at the Jackson/Murray office in 2003.

Lyons was convicted on charges of racketeering and stole more than $4 million from the Anti-Defamation League and other donors with the help of his secret mistress. This money was supposed to go to help rebuild black churches that had been burned to the ground. Lyons also pastored the Bethel Metropolitan Baptist Church in St. Petersburg, Florida. What was the reaction of the congregation to Lyons' arrest? They actually applauded his return to the pulpit after he was bailed out of jail. How did the leaders of the NBC react? They refused to remove him from leadership while the charges were being investigated.

This says to me that the members of Lyons' church and the leadership of the NBC are willing to tolerate illegal conduct from their leaders because they themselves are engaging in conduct that shames the name of Jesus Christ and makes the church a laughingstock. It's difficult to condemn a person for his unethical conduct when you're engaged in immoral conduct yourself. So, instead of repenting from your own immoral behaviors, you make excuses for the immorality of the person who has been caught.

Lyons was protected and honored by his church members, and he was allowed to remain head of the NBC until he was convicted and sent to jail. Of course, just like Cecil Murray, Lyons is a long-time friend of Bill Clinton. Clinton's immoralities—his lying under oath and his adultery—were obviously of little concern to Lyons because he was guilty of his own improper behavior.

The man who was chosen to take Henry Lyons' place as head of Bethel Baptist Church in 2000 was Joaquin Marvin, an associate minister at Greater Union Baptist Church in Pensacola, Florida. The Florida Department of Corrections alerted the congregation that Martin had been sentenced in 1991 to two years of community control on a forgery conviction and had been arrested numerous times from 1986 to 1991 on assault charges, showing a weapon, possession of marijuana and crack cocaine, petty larceny, and violating parole. Yet Bethel Church members voted 200-49 in favor of Martin. Rev. Joseph Harvey, an associate pastor at Bethel, told United Press International at the time, "Everybody at church yesterday was still in favor of him coming. It has been over ten years. His criminal past has no effect on his preaching."[4]

The National Baptist Convention had a dismal history of corrupt leadership even before Lyons took over in 1994. His predecessor was Rev. T.J. Jemison, who put the NBC's power and prestige behind Mike Tyson after he had been charged with raping a young girl in a hotel room. Why? Could it be because Tyson had promised to give the NBC a $5 million gift? Tyson never made good on his promise, but the NBC's credibility was given to Tyson—a man who by all rights should be in a psychiatric care facility. Under Jemison's questionable leadership, the NBC also gave its highest service award to Don King, the boxing promoter, who has been repeatedly under federal investigation for his shady business dealings.[5]

This kind of spiritual corruption within a black church would not have occurred forty years ago. Forty years ago, blacks were ashamed of sin. Personal morality and family togetherness were prized. Love for parents was real, hard work was the norm, and men were strong. The current pathetic state of morality in the black community is a slap in the face to those blacks who suffered and died for our freedoms.

ANTI-AMERICANISM AND RACIST MESSAGES PROMOTED

Black churches have become affiliates of the Democratic party, and most black pastors wink at sin or actively promote sinful behaviors. Black pastors are also guilty of spreading racial hatred through their sermons and by inviting hate-filled leaders into their churches to spread divisiveness and racial tension.

In 2002, for example, the pastor of Salem United Methodist Church in Harlem, New York, allowed Nation of Islam (NOI) racist and anti-American hatemonger Louis Farrakhan to come to his church and give a two-hour speech against America. Farrakhan told the audience that the then-coming war against Iraq was a plot by the Bush administration to wage war on Islam and that blacks must take a leadership role in fighting against the enemies of Allah. He told the assembled, "When I saw the tanks in Tiananmen Square in China, Chinese rolling over their own, I knew that this was being planned against you, here in America."[6]

Farrakhan's anti-American and racist speech was attended by a number of powerful men and women in the entertainment industry as well as Afrocentric racist college professors who support his goals. Among those attending were Def Jam records executive Russell Simmons, rappers Doug E. Fresh and Queen Pen, hip hop pioneer Afrika Bambaata, Dr. Leonard Jeffries, and various Muslim clerics. Dr. Leonard Jeffries, an Afrocentrist professor and professional racist, applauded Farrakhan's speech as one of the most powerful he'd ever heard.

Now why would the pastor of this black church in Harlem allow a known anti-American, anti-white, and anti-Christian bigot to give a speech from his pulpit? The sad truth is that many black pastors have racial attitudes that are no different from those of Farrakhan, whom I consider to be one of the most dangerous men in this nation. I will devote more time to him later, but this incident is just one of dozens of examples of corruption and racial hatred that exist within the black churches of America.[7]

In July 2002, Farrakhan traveled to Iraq and held talks with Abdul Munem Saleh, Saddam Hussein's Islamic Affairs Minister. He was later quoted by the Iraqi news agency as saying, "The Muslim American people are praying to the almighty God to grant victory to Iraq." Farrakhan has since denied saying this, but based on his rabid anti-American past, I have no trouble believing the quote is accurate.[8]

Many black pastors and members of the radical leftist Congressional Black Caucus were opposed to President George W. Bush's efforts to remove Saddam Hussein. These leftists are showing their anti-American and anti-Jewish biases. They're apparently willing to support any regime as long as it's against American interests or security.

Presidential candidate Al Sharpton, for example, was a speaker in January 2003 at an anti-war rally in Washington, D.C., sponsored by ANSWER, a coalition spun off of the Workers World Party, an openly communist group. Who shared the podium with Sharpton?

Congressional Black Caucus leader John Conyers of Michigan gave his support to this rabidly anti-American rally. The paranoid former representative from Georgia, Cynthia McKinney, was also on stage to rant against our war against terrorism.[9]

In February 2003, I invited the co-director of the Los Angeles branch of ANSWER, John Parker, on my daily Information Radio Network (IRN) show to find out exactly what he believed about America and our nation's war on terrorism and Saddam Hussein. Parker refused to tell me if he loved America. I then asked him whom he trusted more, Saddam Hussein or President Bush. After repeatedly asking him this same question, he finally admitted that he trusted Saddam Hussein more than President Bush.

WAR IS NOT THE ANSWER?

On February 8, 2003, black liberal clergy from across the country convened at Detroit's Cobo Hall to address the "State of the Black Union." The event was co-hosted by Bill Clinton–lovers Tavis Smiley and Tom Joyner and was televised by C-SPAN. Notable names in attendance were Rev. Al Sharpton, University of Pennsylvania professor Dr. Michael Eric Dyson, and his wife, Rev. Marcia Louise Dyson.[10]

The general theme of the event was that war with Iraq was unjust. Smiley said, "The *black* point of view about the war is generally not heard in the media." Panelists also noted that major media coverage of the war generally gives the viewers perspectives of *white* men. I've heard of people seeing issues in black and white, but this is ridiculous!

Marcia Louise Dyson praised Louis Farrakhan, saying, "The Nation of Islam has taught us through the works of Minister Farrakhan that we have to take it to the streets. We are responsible for our brothers and for cleaning up our community." She also made this foolish statement: "We cannot say that we are against terrorism in other countries when terrorism exists right here in America."

Al Sharpton said, "To say the war is wrong and wicked is our job as bearers of the truth."

Rev. Dr. James A. Forbes Jr., senior minister at Riverside Church in New York City, stated that if we "ignore the sensibilities of men like Nelson Mandela, then we have a problem." The last time I looked, Nelson Mandela was a communist-socialist pig.

Of course, I had to invite Dr. Forbes to my radio show to ask him about this. Once on the program, he was not much different than most preachers I interview—he wouldn't answer questions directly. He was also very skillful at painting those who saw through his evasions as being extreme.

BOND fully supports President Bush's commitment to fight world-wide Islamic terrorism, and we have been deeply concerned over the future of Israel. I consider Israel to be our spiritual brother, as well as a key, rational democratic partner. If we fail to stand with Israel, I believe America will fail to stand.

Black radicals like Al Sharpton and Cynthia McKinney have long histories of making anti-Jewish statements and taking anti-Jewish actions (I deal with Sharpton's anti-Jewish violence in a later chapter). Jesse Jackson also has a shameful history of vilifying Jews; I vividly recall when Jackson's reference to New York as "Hymie Town" was exposed in the media. Jackson's association with Muslim extremists and the heads of terrorist nations is a matter of public record. Jackson has lent his support to Libya, Yasser Arafat, and Fidel Castro over many decades.

SEXUAL SIN AND ABORTION APPROVED

Many liberal black pastors neglect to teach a moral message to their congregations. Like Cecil Murray at the First AME in Los Angeles, many of them wink at sex outside of marriage and others are openly pro-abortion and pro-homosexual.

In 2000, a group of black church leaders gathered at the National Black Religious Summit IV Sexuality Conference at Howard University School of Divinity in Washington, D.C. The summit was sponsored by the Black Church Initiative, a program of the Religious Coalition for Reproductive Choice.

This group's three-day conference featured pro-abortion advocate and former U.S. Surgeon General Joycelyn Elders. Several hundred pastors and youth leaders from black churches attended.

Elders told these black leaders that "many ministers continue to preach about abstinence. But the vows of abstinence can be broken much easier than a latex condom. Sex has enslaved us all. It has enslaved our ministers to the point that we are ready to kick them out of the church if they speak about sex. We have all been enslaved by myths, taboos and 'isms.'" This disgraceful woman told these pastors that while it's okay to teach about abstinence, they should also teach about "responsible" sexual behavior—in other words, premarital sex with condoms. She also urged them to end discrimination against homosexuals. According to Elders, "Black people know best about discrimination. We need to accept people of all sexual orientations."[11]

Were these pastors not aware that in 1999 Elders had been a guest speaker at the International Sex Worker Foundation for Art, Culture, and Education (a prostitute organization) and had argued for the legalization of prostitution? She told the assembled hookers, "By criminalizing prostitution, we've really criminalized poverty. Many of these women don't have a choice about this because their choice is whether they want to eat or starve to death."[12]

In 2002, Elders wrote the introduction to *Harmful to Minors* by Judith Levine. In her book, Levine argues that children should be free to have sex with adults if they wish to do so. Her book is widely praised by children's liberationists, and pedophiles have been given yet another "academic" book that justifies the sexual molestation of children.

In her introduction, Elders says that Levine's book exposes "the influence of the religious right (or what I have been known to call the 'very religious non-Christian right')." She continues, "I have spoken and written many times about my disgust with people who have a love affair with the fetus but won't take care of children once they are born."[13]

This is a woman who, while serving as our surgeon general under Bill Clinton, called for public schools to teach boys and girls how to masturbate as part of their sex education lessons.

And several hundred black pastors and youth leaders listened to her at this pro-condom, pro-abortion, and pro-homosexual conference at a black school of divinity!

BLACKS NEED ROLE MODELS, NOT LEADERS

How does a person become easy prey for corrupt leaders like these? It starts in the home. He is set up to fail by parents who themselves were set up to fail. They have passed on their sins. A child is tempted to hate his parents by their often poor example. When the child falls to hating, he loses his objectivity and becomes blind. He then becomes subject to corrupt leaders instead of to the reason and common sense he was born with.

At one time, children grew up believing in God and loving and respecting their parents because they were respectable. Many of today's children, particularly in the black community, do not believe in God and do not love their parents. They instead believe in leaders who know how to bring out their rage and justify it. This is why blacks are so heavily anti-war and anti-American. These leaders are expert at redirecting the people's rage at the targets of their choice. They are skillful manipulators and are the true enemies of black Americans. This is why I maintain that blacks don't need leaders. What they do need, however, are good role models. They need role models who will inform them about the truth of our nation—the greatest in the world—and its heritage of freedom. America is imperfect, of course, but it has been the beacon of freedom to millions of individuals throughout our history.

There are an estimated thirteen million illegal aliens in this nation right now, and more are arriving each day. Do other nations have such a problem with men, women, and children trying to get into their countries? No. In many Muslim, communist, and African nations, people are trying to flee from tyranny to live in the freedom provided by Western democracies. They want what we have.

There is also a false idea being perpetuated in the black community that the political leaders we elect must be black. I wholeheartedly object to such a notion. The most important aspect in a good leader is character. When I go to the polls, I choose candidates with character, regardless of whether they are black or white. Character, not color, is what counts.

Blacks must learn that true freedom from poverty is available only through hard work and perseverance, not through affirmative action programs, protesting, or blind allegiance to the Democratic party. Progress can only be made when blacks throw off the oppression of their civil rights leaders and learn to stand on their own.

The key to the future for blacks is a commitment to America and its ideals of freedom, personal responsibility, the free enterprise system, and moral principles.

These are the principles we're teaching the young men who are in our Home for Boys and to the boys who are involved in BOND's After School Character Programs. We teach these young men that they have to take responsibility for their own lives and not be dependent upon others to do their thinking for them. We teach independence, not dependence, and it works! This nation is all about self-reliance, not blind obedience to a leader who frequently has his or her own personal agenda. That agenda may be one of control, money, or gaining power over another person's life. We teach our students that no man is to be their master. This is true freedom, and it allows these young men to become successful adults.

One of our recent graduates from our Home for Boys came to us several years ago. He had come from a single-parent home. His father had died; he was becoming a rebellious and uncontrollable child, so his mother brought him to us. While enrolled in our program, he became a disk jockey, became self-controlled, and quit blaming other people for his own problems. He's learned that the white man is not responsible for his difficulties. He's also realized that there are good and bad people in every race. He has learned to judge people, as Dr. Martin Luther King Jr. so eloquently said, by the content of their character, not the color of their skin. I have no doubt that he will do well in life.

When he first came to us, he said that he'd always wanted to start a business but thought the white man would hold him back. He also didn't think he had enough money to start a business. We showed him a simple and inexpensive way of getting his business started. We taught him basic principles about hard work and providing a product that others wanted.

We see the successes of these principles every day in the young men who are involved in our program. They learn valuable skills; but one of the most important things they learn in the program is to change the way they think about whites, their own failings, and their future hopes and dreams. I've found that no one can keep you down if you take responsibility for your own life and don't waste your time blaming others for whatever problems may have come your way.

BOOKER T. WASHINGTON: ROLE MODEL FOR BLACKS

We use *Up from Slavery* by Booker T. Washington as one of the primary textbooks in our After School Character Building Program. Sadly, most blacks have little knowledge about Washington and his vision for blacks during the last half of the 19th century and the early 20th century. Yet his story is one that should inspire blacks and whites to push for excellence and for racial reconciliation in our nation.

Washington's legacy is unappreciated in this day and age when black rage and blame are all that seem to matter to those self-appointed black leaders who routinely get face time on TV talk shows and on radio to vent their hatred of whites and our economic system.

Booker T. Washington, however, had a common-sense approach to black progress and integration into American society. He believed that blacks needed to have both vocational training and a sound education. He taught that a person could become free and independent if he had skills working with his hands as well as intellectual knowledge for a professional position. The person equipped with both physical skills and a good education is prepared for anything. It is my hope one day to establish an academy for boys that will implement Washington's vision.

Booker Taliaferro was the son of an unknown white man and a slave of James Burroughs, a farmer in Virginia. Later, when his mother, Jane, married another slave named Washington Ferguson, he became known as Booker T. Washington.

At the age of nine, Washington found employment as a salt packer. He later worked in coal mines and eventually became a houseboy for the wife of Lewis Ruffed, the owner of the mines. This woman encouraged Washington to pursue an education, and in 1872, he entered the Hampton Agricultural Institute.

While at Hampton, Washington worked late into the night as a janitor in order to pay his room and board. In his autobiography, he wrote, "I gladly accepted [the job] because it was a place where I could work out nearly all the cost of my board. The work was hard and taxing, but I stuck to it. I had a large number of rooms to care for, and had to work late into the night, while at the same time I had to rise by four o'clock in the morning, in order to build the fires and have a little time in which to prepare my lessons."[14]

At Hampton, Washington said he learned to love work, "not alone for its financial value, but for labor's own sake and for the independence and self-reliance which the ability to do something which the world wants brings."[15]

Samuel Armstrong was the principal of this school. He had been the commander of black troops during the Civil War and became Washington's mentor. In *Up from Slavery*, Washington described Armstrong as "a great man—the noblest rarest human being it has ever been my privilege to meet."[16]

Armstrong believed in instilling character and morality into his students and also believed that blacks needed a practical education if they were to compete in the marketplace. Armstrong's philosophy was to have a lasting impact on Washington in later years.

In 1888, with the advice and encouragement of Armstrong, Washington became head of the Tuskegee Negro Normal Institute. The Institute taught academic subjects but emphasized a practical or industrial education. Students were taught farming, carpentry, masonry, shoemaking, printing, and cabinetry. The school began in a small rundown building owned by a local church, but with the skills the students learned, they actually helped to build a larger facility on 540 acres of land. Under Washington's direction, 400 students received a good education and learned practical skills they could use the rest of their lives.

Washington's advice has been an inspiration to me and to the young men who take part in our outreach through BOND. His belief in hard work freed him from any victim mentality or hatred of whites. He once said, "I have learned that success is to be measured not so much by the position that one has reached in life as by the obstacles which he has overcome while trying to succeed." He also chastised those who blame others for their failures: "I have never had much patience with the multitudes of people who are always ready to explain why one cannot succeed. I have always had high regard for the man who could tell me how to succeed."[17]

Washington's ideas about working hard, learning practical skills, and teaching racial peace proved to be of benefit to hundreds of black students who went through the Tuskegee Institute. But then as now, there were radical blacks who hated any black man who dared to teach blacks to be productive and independent.

The leftist movement of blacks was led by W.E.B. DuBois, who became Washington's harshest critic and an enemy of true black freedom. DuBois graduated from Fisk University in Nashville, Tennessee, in 1888 and received his doctorate from Harvard University in 1895. He decided early on in his career that the only route for blacks to gain progress was through agitation and protest.

His views clashed with those of Washington who was urging blacks to elevate themselves through hard work. DuBois targeted Washington as the enemy of black progress in his 1903 book, *The Souls of Black Folk*. DuBois charged that Washington was leading blacks back into oppression, not freedom from it.

In 1905, DuBois helped found the Niagara Movement in direct opposition to Washington's proposals for black progress. He later helped found the NAACP and became the group's researcher and editor of its magazine *Crisis*. As head of this magazine, the NAACP became Booker T. Washington's main enemy and critic.

DuBois was also enamored of black nationalism and socialism, which took the form of Pan-Africanism. He believed that African blacks and American blacks needed to work together for freedom from white oppression. He urged separate black literature and art and promoted the idea of separate black cooperatives based on a socialist model. The Afrocentrist movement on our college campuses is the result of DuBois' efforts to divide Americans into black and white enclaves, rather than promoting the colorblind society later envisioned by Dr. Martin Luther King Jr.

DuBois' growing hatred of America and the free enterprise system led him to be identified with pro-Russian causes in the late 1940s and early 1950s. In 1951 he was indicted as an unregistered agent of a foreign power but was acquitted by a federal judge. His hatred of America became so intense that he joined the Communist party in 1961, moved to Ghana, and renounced his American citizenship. A writer for *Atlantic Monthly*, who visited him in Ghana shortly before his death in 1963, described his home as being adorned with busts of Marx, Lenin, and Mao Tse-tung. These men were responsible for the brutal deaths of millions of people over the past century—yet they were revered by DuBois. His writings and philosophy have done untold damage to black progress in this nation.[18]

Booker T. Washington promoted racial harmony, black business enterprise, vocational education, and strong Christian black families. DuBois, however, agitated for government handouts and racial separatism. Unfortunately, DuBois' spirit lives on in the modern day "civil rights movement."

I encounter this spirit in churches, on TV and radio, and on college campuses where I frequently speak.* I gave a speech at Penn State in late 2002 for the College Republicans organization on campus. Several angry students who identified themselves as members of the college Black Caucus came to hear my speech and began delivering a series of diatribes against me during the Q&A session.

One young woman stood up and shouted at me that she deserved

---

*The Jesse Lee Peterson TV show is broadcast nationally and worldwide by God's Learning Channel (www.GodsLearningChannel.com). The Jesse Lee Peterson Radio Show is nationally syndicated by Information Radio Network (IRN, www.InfoRadioNet.com).

reparations because she wouldn't be here in America if it weren't for slavery. She yelled that America was a racist society and that capitalism was the enemy of blacks. She kept screaming uncontrollably and refused to let me respond to any of her accusations. Other radical blacks eventually stood up and began shouting at me. One of them looked like he was coming toward the podium to physically attack me. They all indicated their hatred for America.

These radical blacks attempted to hijack the Q&A session of our meeting and behaved in a shameful and uncivilized manner. If they had looked beyond their own misplaced rage, they might have learned something useful.

Unless there is a radical change in these young blacks' attitudes about America and the free enterprise system, they are likely to spend the remainder of their lives as angry racists who hate America and the only economic system that allows people to become as successful as they wish.

Unfortunately, there is a virulent strain of anti-capitalism and anti-Americanism that runs throughout all of the black power and civil rights groups. Many of the so-called black leaders are socialists, but they hide their true philosophy by calling themselves "progressives." The Congressional Black Caucus, for example, is filled with blacks who are also members of the Progressive Caucus, a group affiliated with the Democratic Socialists of America. This group is an offshoot of the Socialist International.[19] These individuals despise free enterprise and favor a government that will control every aspect of our lives. These men and women want welfare dependence and the control of individuals. Because of their foolish philosophy, they routinely oppose any efforts that might provide blacks with true freedom or encourage independence and productivity.

2

The New "Massa"s

—⚬—

*Remember the story of Jim Jones? Blacks have
been "drinking the Kool-Aid" for years*

My encounter with the hostile anti-capitalist and racist blacks in the Black Caucus at Penn State made me more concerned than ever about the danger of blacks turning their lives over to a racist leader or to a foreign ideology that causes them to hate America, whites, and the free-enterprise system. Those students have fallen victim to corrupt leaders who teach them to hate and teach them to obey blindly. They face a dismal and hopeless future.

What has happened to many blacks in America today is precisely what happened to the naïve followers of cultist Jim Jones. What he did to his followers is reflected in what Jesse Jackson, Louis Farrakhan, Al Sharpton, and others are doing to blacks today.

In Guyana on November 18, 1978, 913 followers of cult leader Jim Jones gathered together at their People's Temple camp. Then they began passing around cyanide-laced Kool-Aid as part of a mass suicide pact ordered by Jones. The brainwashed followers of this delusional cult leader began by giving this poison to their children, and then they took it themselves. They died agonizing deaths. When it was over, hundreds of bodies lay in heaps around this jungle compound.

The followers of Jim Jones—mostly black—had moved with him to Guyana from San Francisco, California, to flee from America and to practice their peculiar religion in obscurity and freedom. These were well-meaning people who wanted to worship God in their own way, but they were eventually turned into slaves by Jim Jones' charismatic personality and teaching. They gradually lost the ability to think on their own and turned their wills and minds over to the leadership of that one man. Eventually, they lost all reason and blindly obeyed whatever Jones told them to do. This brainwashing process took Jones years to accomplish, but he ultimately had the power of life and death over his mental slaves. The majority of his followers willingly died for him when he told them to drink from the poisoned cup.

This same brainwashing process has slowly—but surely—put millions of black Americans under the mind control of corrupt civil rights leaders, legislators, black journalists, and leftist black preachers. What these unscrupulous black leaders have done is create a cult of "blackness." They have successfully put blacks into a trance-like state by constantly repeating the mantra of "racism" to get them to obey blindly. The R-word is used over and over again to link conservatives, whites, or Republicans to racism and the supposed hatred of blacks. It doesn't matter how absurd the linkage might be. During the 2000 election, for example, the NAACP ran an anti-Bush campaign ad in Texas that linked Republicans to the dragging death of black man James Byrd. This dishonest attempt to link George W. Bush with the killing of a black man by hateful bigots undoubtedly worked with many blacks in the nation.

In Florida, during the 2000 post-election recount debacle, Democratic National Committee Chairman Terry McAuliffe, aided by Jesse Jackson and Al Sharpton, spread the fiction that blacks had been harassed or discouraged from voting at the polls. This was untrue. Black columnist Clarence Page noted shortly after the election that blacks actually voted in increased numbers—up to 15 percent of the voting population compared to 10 percent in 1996. According to Page, there was a "scarcity of actual intimidation, harassment or fraud, despite probes by the U.S. Justice Department, the NAACP, and other voting-rights organizations." Page says that whatever problems actually did occur among black voters were due to the unusually high turnout at the polls. Yet McAuliffe and his minions continue to spout these lies designed to create hatred between blacks and the Republican party.[1]

The deceivers who run the racial hatred industry in our nation have given blacks the poisoned Kool-Aid of racism, conspiratorial paranoia, abortion, ebonics, critical race theory, a phony Afrocentric view of history, sexual immorality, anti-capitalist and socialistic ideas, and a hatred of successful black conservatives. This powerful and poisonous mixture has done incredible damage to race relations and to black progress in this nation.

THE KOOL-AID OF HATE AGAINST BLACK CONSERVATIVES

One thing that black liberals hate more than whites or white conservatives is a black conservative like me. The hate-filled rhetoric used to vilify, marginalize, or destroy black conservatives is something to behold. Black liberals despise individuals who are independent and free-thinking, but I refuse to be brought back to the Democratic party plantation to be used as a pawn for the leftist, immoral agendas of liberal politicians.

The ridicule of U.S. Supreme Court Justice Clarence Thomas has gone on for years and has clearly revealed just how hateful these black liberals can be.

I have met Justice Thomas. While I was in the Capitol some years back, I had the incredible honor of speaking with this great American in his chambers for an hour and a half. It was truly one of the great experiences of my lifetime and one I'll never forget.

Justice Thomas gave a speech several years ago entitled "A New Era for Black Leadership." In it, he described how liberal blacks decided to begin vilifying any black who dared leave the Democratic party plantation:

> Our black counterparts on the Left and in the Democratic party assured our [black conservatives] alienation. Those of us who were identified as conservative were ignored at best. We were treated with disdain, regularly castigated, and mocked; and of course we could be accused of anything without recourse and with impunity.
>
> . . . The flames were further fanned by the media. I often felt that the media assumed that, to be black, one had to espouse leftist ideas and Democratic politics. Any black who deviated from the ideological litany of requisites was an oddity and was to be cut from the herd and attacked. Hence, any disagreement we had with black Democrats or those on the Left was exaggerated. Our character and motives were impugned and challenged by the same reporters who supposedly were writing objective stories.[2]

The black liberals' hatred for Clarence Thomas is stunning. Instead of honoring him for rising from abject poverty in a world of discrimination to become a U.S. Supreme Court Justice, they ridicule him—one even openly wished he would die an early death. Here is a sample of the kinds of hate speech that have been directed against this fine, patriotic man by black liberals:

> I hope [Thomas's] wife feeds him lots of eggs and butter, and he dies early, like many black men do, of heart disease. . . . He's an absolutely reprehensible person.
>
> —*Columnist Julianne Malveaux*[3]

> [Thomas has] ethnically ceased being an African American.
>
> —*Dr. Manning Marable*[4]

> [I]f you give Thomas a little flour on his face, you'd think you had [former Klansman] David Duke.
>
> —*The late columnist Carl Rowan*[5]

I have told [Thomas] I am ashamed of him, because he is becoming to the black community what Benedict Arnold was to the nation he deserted; and what Judas Iscariot was to Jesus: a traitor; and what Brutus was to Caesar: an assassin.

—*Rev. Joseph Lowery of the Southern Christian Leadership Conference*[6]

Thomas, of course, has replied to these charges over the years with dignity. He has said:

Long gone is the time when we [blacks] opposed the notion that we all looked alike and talked alike. [But] somehow we have come to exalt the new black stereotype above all and demand conformity to that norm. . . . [However], I assert my right to think for myself, to refuse to have my ideas assigned to me as though I was an intellectual slave because I'm black.[7]

Justice Thomas is not the only black conservative to be attacked because of his beliefs. Liberal blacks have also aimed their attacks at the distinguished conservative black activist Ward Connerly, who successfully led the 1996 battle in California to overturn racial preferences in state hiring and contracts through Proposition 209. Jesse Jackson has called Connerly a "house slave" and a "puppet of the white man."[8]

The NAACP's radical leader Julian Bond has referred to Connerly as a "fraud" and a "con man." Bond has also leveled his hate speech at all black conservatives and has accused them of being part of a "right-wing conspiracy" of "hustlers and hucksters." According to Bond, conservative blacks are ventriloquist "dummies" who speak "in their puppet master's voice."[9]

Richard Dixon, a black writer for the web site *Black Oklahoma Today,* penned an article not long ago entitled "Traitors within Our Ranks: Thoughts on How Black Conservatism Contributes to the State of Racism in This Country." According to Dixon, black conservatism is a "tool of racism" that is being wielded by a "strong right wing agenda" that is designed to dismantle all aspects of the civil rights movement. Dixon targets his vitriolic attacks at such brilliant black conservative writers as Dr. Walter E. Williams, Thomas Sowell, and Shelby Steele. In Dixon's strange and delusional world, these writers simply reflect a "white elitist perspective" that "further lights the fires of racial discrimination against blacks and other ethnic minorities."[10]

Dixon makes the absurd claim that the Republican party's ultimate goal is to exclude millions of blacks and other ethnic minorities from achieving full participation in American society, economically, politically, and culturally. He also claims that the goal of Republicans is to dismantle all civil rights laws and programs.

Dixon's rantings are typical of the kind of delusional thinking that goes on inside the heads of black radicals. Leftist blacks like Dixon live in a paranoid world where all whites are considered enemies, conservatives are plotting to destroy the black race through AIDS and crack cocaine, and Republicans want to send blacks back to the plantations and deny them civil rights.

Unfortunately, far too many blacks believe such nonsense and these racists continue to make millions off the donations of their naïve followers. They need to heed the advice of Clarence Thomas who refuses to allow self-proclaimed black leaders to think for him or to demand conformity from him.

In late 2002, black entertainer Harry Belafonte took aim at Secretary of State Colin Powell by calling him a "house slave" to President George W. Bush. According to Belafonte, "There's an old saying in the days of slavery [sic]. There are those slaves on the plantation and there were those slaves who lived in the big house. You got the privilege of living in the house to serve the master. Colin Powell was permitted to come into the house of the master."

Belafonte also accused Bush's National Security Advisor Condoleezza Rice of turning her back on blacks. He said he considers Rice to be even worse than Powell because she has allegedly failed to make more "lenient" or "appropriate" public comments about blacks than Powell has. Rice responded to his smear against her by telling CNN's Larry King, "If Harry Belafonte disagrees with my political views, that's fine. That's a conversation that is worth having. We're Americans. Everybody should be able to debate views. But I don't need Harry Belafonte to tell me what it means to be black."[11]

Of course, Jesse Jackson also had to jump into this controversy by adding his anti-black conservative thoughts: "I'd like to see both [Powell] and Condoleezza Rice show some moral backbone, show some courage, show some commitment to principles that are far higher than those being espoused by their boss."[12]

Continuing the attack against Condoleezza Rice, a liberal talk show host in Florida created a musical parody of Rice and released it on CD. The title is "Kiss a Nigger Good Morning." The CD cover has a picture of Bush greeting Mrs. Rice with a social kiss.

This is shameful. It shows how desperate liberals are to keep blacks in bondage to Democratic politics. It also shows that you just can't win with liberals. If President Bush had not appointed Powell and Rice to two of the highest positions in his administration, he would have been trashed for being racially insensitive and anti-black. However, once he did appoint them, along with other minorities, to powerful positions within his administration, liberals trashed these individuals as being Uncle Toms and house slaves, appointed only to do the master's bidding.

The totalitarian civil rights leaders do not want free-thinking, independent blacks. They want Jonestown-type followers who will blindly obey, donate their money to liberal extremist causes, and vote a straight Democratic ticket. I reject this dictatorial control over my life, and I am working to convince others to throw off this cult-like hold that liberals have over blacks.

THE KOOL-AID OF PARANOIA

In my opinion, one of the most vicious anti-white conspiracy-mongers in America is Maxine Waters, a congresswoman from Los Angeles. Waters is a former head of the Congressional Black Caucus and has a long history of fomenting racial discontent and paranoia among blacks. She is also an enemy of blacks who dare to espouse conservative values and think for themselves.

Waters has been involved for years in spreading the false story that the Central Intelligence Agency was responsible for introducing crack cocaine into the inner city in Los Angeles and elsewhere. Along with Joe Madison, an NAACP board member, and Nation of Islam leader Louis Farrakhan, Waters began spreading this hate-filled nonsense back in 1996, and her false claims are still posted on her congressional website (www.House.gov/Waters).

This professional agitator and her racist allies grabbed on to an exposé published by the *San Jose Mercury News* that claimed that the CIA had used drug money from cocaine sales in the inner cities of America to help fund the resistance to the pro-communist Sandinistas in Nicaragua. The article, "Dark Alliance," written by Gary Webb, was later discredited by Reed Irvine's Accuracy in Media (AIM) organization. AIM demonstrated that Webb misquoted sources and ignored other evidence that proved his theories wrong about any CIA-drug connection in the inner cities.

The AIM report exposing Webb's story was published in October 1996, but this didn't deter Waters from demanding a congressional investigation and holding seminars where she railed against this alleged CIA conspiracy to destroy the black race and, in effect, destroy our nation as well with the spread of drugs into our communities.[13]

Waters is still unconvinced that there is no such thing as a CIA-drug conspiracy to destroy blacks, even though such a conspiracy is logically inconsistent. Why would a government agency introduce a socially destructive drug into our inner cities? Such an effort would bring ruin upon our cities, increase crime rates, and result in serious social problems.

Black racist leaders like Spike Lee and Louis Farrakhan have also spread the falsehood that AIDS was created to kill black people. Lee has claimed that "AIDS is a government-engineered disease." This conspiracy theory has even been accepted by Bill Cosby, who once claimed that AIDS was "started by human beings to get after certain people they don't like."[14]

Lee, of course, is a famous black racist who is known for his disdain of interracial marriages. He once said, "I give interracial couples a look. Daggers. They get uncomfortable when they see me on the street." Several years ago, Lee publicly declared that he only wanted to be interviewed by black reporters.

A survey conducted by two social scientists in 1995 among 1,000 black church members found that 35 percent believed that AIDS was created to destroy blacks and 30 percent would not rule it out.[15] Another survey done in 1999 still found 25 percent of blacks believing that AIDS is a man-made virus against blacks. Another 23 percent indicated they were still undecided.[16]

Who wins when black racists generate such paranoia about drugs and AIDS within the black community? Why, the black racists, of course. Their allies in government can be easily convinced to dole out millions in "AIDS education" for blacks or to distribute condoms.

Louis Farrakhan also wins more anti-American and anti-white converts among people who can be convinced that AIDS is a white man's plot against all blacks.

Instead of blaming sexual immorality and drug use for the spread of AIDS or irresponsible behavior for spreading crack cocaine in inner cities, black racist leaders use these convenient conspiracy theories to absolve blacks from personal responsibility for their actions and convince them that whites are their enemies.

THE KOOL-AID OF AFROCENTRISM AND CRITICAL RACE THEORY

Among some of the most dangerous racist notions being promoted among blacks today are the concepts of Afrocentrism and critical race theory. Both of these belief systems create hatred of whites and even go so far as to reject "reality" as being socially constructed by different racial groups.

Afrocentrism is being promoted in our nation's colleges by radical leftist and America-hating black professors who have invented a fictional history of Africa and its influence in world civilization.

Time magazine exposed the lunacy of Afrocentric education in its March 4, 1994, issue. The exposé was aptly titled "Teaching Reverse Racism: A strange doctrine of black superiority is finding its way into schools and colleges."

The author noted some of the major tenets of Afrocentrism, including the belief that Egyptians were black and mastered flight with gliders, that they invented electric batteries, and that their dark pigmentation (melanin) "not only made them more humane and superior to lighter-colored people in body and mind but also provided such paranormal powers as ESP and psychokinesis."

The *Washington Times* (March 3, 1996) also described some of the other wild claims of Afrocentrists: that Africans sailed to America thousands of years before Columbus and that the first human life, first religion, first philosophy, first mathematics, and first science came out of Africa. Afrocentrists also claim that Napoleon deliberately shot off the nose of the Sphinx and other statues in order to hide the fact that Egyptians were black.

Very few whites or blacks have had the courage to challenge Afrocentric studies in our nation's universities, but one professor did: Mary Lefkowitz, a professor who teaches the Greek classics at Wellesley. In response to the growing trend of Afrocentrist fiction taught as fact, she wrote *Not Out of Africa: How Afrocentrism Became An Excuse To Teach Myth As History.*[17]

In her book, she thoroughly debunks the major tenets of Afrocentrism. In an interview in the *Washington Times* about her book, she notes, "Afrocentrism not only teaches what is untrue; it encourages students to ignore chronology, to forget about looking for material evidence, to select only those facts that are convenient, and to invent facts whenever useful or necessary."[18]

She continues, "There's nothing black or white about it [Afrocentrism]. We're talking historical issues. Yes, people are afraid of being called racist, but one should always stand up for accuracy in history. I don't want to see indoctrination of any kind in schools."

As Lefkowitz has said, Afrocentrism teaches myth as history. This does a great disservice to black college students who take these courses and come away with an entirely fictional view of history and race. Afrocentrism creates paranoia and a belief in racial superiority based on myths. Black students who graduate with such ideas will be greatly hindered in their lives because they've been taught lies.

Afrocentrism myths taught as truth are deeply embedded within the black studies departments at hundreds of universities throughout the United States and the world. Black racists get away with their fictional portrayals of African history because most whites are too afraid to challenge them for fear of being called racists.

Black leftists have a love affair with Africa because down deep they really hate whites, Christianity, American civilization, and capitalism. They prefer tribalism, black dictatorships, and socialist economies.

One black who once idealized Africa is Keith Richburg, a former foreign correspondent for the *Washington Post*. Richburg spent three years in Africa covering Somalia, Rwanda, and South Africa. He eagerly accepted this assignment because he wanted to connect with his African roots and heritage.

After spending three years observing the horrors of African dictatorships and the cruelty dealt out by African warlords and tribesmen, he came back to the United States with a renewed love of freedom and gratitude that his ancestors had been brought to America in slave ships. In his book, *Out of America: A Black Man Confronts Africa* Richburg said he was truly grateful for living in America: "Let me drop the charade and put it as simply as I know how: there but for the grace of God go I. . . . I thank God my ancestor survived that voyage [in a slave ship]."[19]

Richburg described what became a defining moment for him in his realization that Africa was a continent filled with violence and bloodshed. He recalled standing on a bridge over the Kagera River in Rwanda watching corpses slowly fall over a waterfall and float downriver. He wrote: "They move slowly, in eerie procession through the river's murky water, twisting in the current, sometimes banging against rocks. One is wearing red underpants. Many have their hands tied behind their backs. Some, if not most, are missing limbs, or a head. . . ."[20]

Richburg also noted his disgust when covering a meeting in Africa where Jesse Jackson and other black Americans "heaped a nauseating outpouring of praise on some of Africa's most brutal and corrupt strongmen" in a display of "the complete ignorance about Africa among America's so-called black elite."[21]

Yet this is the Africa that is idealized by Afrocentrists who teach lies to naïve black college students. They are miseducating generation after generation of blacks to believe myths as history!

A philosophy as equally absurd and dangerous to educated blacks is critical race theory. Critical race theory is a post-modern belief that there is no such thing as objective reality. It promotes the lie that each race has its own version of reality and that there may never be true racial harmony because of the existence of these multiple realities.

Only a liberal college professor could believe such nonsense, and that's why it's flourishing on our nation's college campuses and our nation's law schools. Anthony Cook, for example, is a black law professor at Georgetown University Law School. He teaches civil rights and race relations law. He is a promoter of critical race theory. He explains it this way: "Critical race theory wants to bring race to the very center of the analysis of most situations. Its assumption is that race has affected our perception of reality and our understanding of the world in almost every way."[22]

Critical race theorists claim that our judicial system is so infected with racism that blacks cannot ever receive a fair trial because of competing views of reality. Paul Butler, a black professor at George Washington University, believes in critical race theory and has urged black juries to acquit all blacks charged in nonviolent drug crimes. In cases involving blacks stealing the property of whites, Butler says juries should determine whether or not a guilty verdict will help or harm blacks, not whether the person is actually guilty. Butler believes this is a kind of black self-help effort—payback for decades of white oppression. In short, critical race theorists aren't concerned about justice in criminal trials; they're only concerned about protecting blacks.[23]

One critic of this dangerous legal theory is Suzanna Sherry, who has written a book called *Beyond All Reason*. Sherry notes, "The problem with denying any objective reality is that there is no way of mediating among the competing perceptions of reality except power. And what they ultimately want is more power for their perceptions."[24]

Critical race theorists reject using facts to argue their cases. Instead, they make up stories or fables to make their points. The truth of a statement doesn't matter to these people. The issue is one of power and winning over an opponent. The goal is to achieve a so-called "black" view of reality over "white" views.

What we can expect to see in the future from this absurd theory is more cases of injustice in our legal system as black juries deliberately free the guilty as a way of expressing solidarity with the "black community" from white racism. Black criminals will go free to commit other crimes, and their victims will never receive the justice they deserve. This can only increase racial tensions and distrust.

THE KOOL-AID OF EBONICS

Robert L. Williams, a former professor of psychology at Washington University, invented the term *ebonics,* which is a combination of the words *ebony* and *phonics*. Williams says he coined ebonics in 1973 "because [I] was sick and tired of white folks writing about the [learning] deficiencies of African-Americans." Williams claims that ebonics is a legitimate language and should be promoted as such in our schools.[25]

In 1997, the Oakland School Board made national headlines with its plan to encourage black students to speak ebonics as a legitimate language. It also recommended that ebonics receive the same kind of federal funding provided for Spanish and Asian-speaking students. Fortunately, the public outcry against this idiocy was immediate. (Five months after deciding to promote ebonics, the Oakland School Board became so embarrassed that it rescinded its proposal.)

During this controversy, I went to Sacramento and testified against ebonics before a California Senate Committee, and I was criticized by black radicals who supported it.

I had been named the Southern California director of "Stop

'Ebonics'/Save Our Children," an organization opposed to gutter language disguised as "black speech." I, along with my friend Ezola Foster and others, testified at the California State Senate Education Committee in Sacramento, at the request of California State Senator Raymond Haynes. Senator Haynes authored a bill which would prevent any state monies from funding ebonics instruction in California schools.

My presentation proved to be brief and quite eventful. I began by saying that there is no such thing as ebonics. "This is just another attempt by people like Jesse Jackson, Maxine Waters, the Oakland School Board"— I then turned and looked right at Diane Watson, who is an influential black leader and was a state senator at the time—"and Diane Watson to control black people, and keep them down for their own personal gain."

Diane Watson jumped out of her chair. "How dare you!" she ranted, saying, "Turn his microphone off." My microphone indeed was turned off, and our side was prevented from finishing our testimony.

During the ruckus I was also told by the chairman of the committee, Senator Leroy Greene, "Your comments are outrageous, sir; you're through for the day." "I am ashamed that you would insult a black lady of great esteem," chimed in fellow Democrat Teresa Hughes of Los Angeles. "She's no lady!" I quickly replied.

Senator Watson demanded an apology from me, but I refused. "Remove him, sergeant! How dare he come up here and defame me!" Senator Greene decided not to follow this demand. As I got up to return to my seat, Watson again demanded an apology, this time in writing. I pointed at her, saying, "She owes black America an apology. I don't owe her an apology!" Again, she began to scream, "Sergeant, put him out!" But the chairman would not do it.

The committee meeting broke up shortly after, but not before the committee voted eight to three against our side. By this time, nearly all sense of order had been lost. To his credit, Senator Haynes stuck by me. Some of the media tried to make it appear that I had helped lose the vote by "insulting a [committee] member." Senator Haynes and others in attendance knew better. Seven "aye" votes were needed for passage, and our side had three. There was no real chance in a liberal Democrat-controlled committee to pass this bill.

This incident is really a good illustration of what happens when you have a group of elites who rule for some forty years. They want to be able to freely quash all dissent without challenge.

I recall that when fighting against Proposition 209 (to eliminate affirmative action in California state facilities and institutions), the same Diane Watson was not content to stick to the issues. She attacked Proposition 209's author, Ward Connerly, for being married to a white woman.[26]

Watson currently represents the 33rd district in Los Angeles in the U.S. House of Representatives, where she is a member of the leftist Congressional Black Caucus and the Progressive Caucus (a group of socialists in the House of Representatives). She now has a national platform to push her hatred of whites and her crazy left-wing political agendas.

Ebonics is not a separate language. It is ghetto speech and substandard English. To claim that ebonics is a positive way of communicating for blacks is to condemn blacks to menial jobs and economic inferiority. A person who fails to learn correct language skills is forever handicapped in seeking employment.

It is disturbing that during the Oakland School Board debate over ebonics, black church leaders in California came to the defense of this defective and substandard speech for black children. The California Conference Ministerial Alliance of the African Methodist Episcopal Church issued a resolution in February 1997 in total support of ebonics. It also indicated that its AME churches would help promote ebonics through afterschool programs, spelling bees, and essay development projects.

According to the AME leaders, the churches would be used to "implement social action efforts in which the church becomes a space for transformation" by encouraging young black children to practice ebonics.

Instead of providing strong leadership and encouraging black children to learn standard English, the politically correct leaders of the AME have sided with the Afrocentrists to promote ghetto speech to black kids. With so-called spiritual leaders such as these, it is little wonder that many black children fare so poorly in school.

Another destructive idea promoted by the problem profiteers is the belief that educational achievement is a "white value" that must be rejected by self-respecting blacks. This anti-educational belief is widely held by black students in our nation's public schools. The decent and hardworking black student who does his homework, speaks proper English, and gets good grades is frequently ridiculed and scorned by other black students. The high-achieving black student is looked upon as a race traitor or an Oreo who has adopted the white man's attitudes about success and hard work.

This tragic and self-destructive attitude among black students is clearly evident in colleges. John McWhorter is a black man, a linguistics professor at UC Berkeley, and the author of *Losing the Race: Self-Sabotage in Black America*. According to McWhorter, the biggest problem facing blacks in America is not racism but self-sabotage and an ideology of victimology and anti-intellectualism.

McWhorter claims that low black educational achievements are not the result of racism but of an attitude within the black community that academic achievement is a "white thing" and that blacks must reject such efforts in order to stay "culturally black."

He says in his book that he consistently finds black students to be lazy and uncaring in the work they produce. "I have found it impossible to avoid nothing less than fearing that a black student in my class is likely to be a problem case. We are trained to say at this point that I am stereotyping, but I have come to expect this for the simple reason that it has been true, class after class, year after year."[27]

As long as high academic achievements are considered a "white thing" by black students, we will continue to have blacks being educational failures as well as being problematic for society. McWhorter, of course, has been smeared by black racists as a "rent-a-black person" because he has had the courage to tell the truth.

Racial hucksters continue to rail against the "system" as the cause of poor black performance in schools. Yet the biggest problem may be the self-destructive attitude that getting good grades is a white value that must be rejected by all blacks.

THE KOOL-AID OF KWANZAA

One of the most incredible examples of how black leaders are exploiting the race is by promoting the "holiday" Kwanzaa.

Most whites are fearful of telling the truth about Kwanzaa because they'll be labeled racist, anti-black, and intolerant. Hate-filled men like Ron Karenga, however, have used this bogus holiday to preach Afrocentrism, anti-white views, and collectivism.

In 1966, Ron Karenga created Kwanzaa, a holiday that allegedly helps blacks to get in touch with their African roots. At the time, Karenga was also the head of United Slaves Organization (USO), a Marxist "black power" group that was a rival to the Black Panther party. USO members and Black Panther terrorists frequently got involved in violent confrontations and several people died as a result.

In 1970, Karenga and two of his followers were arrested and charged with conspiracy and assault in the torture of Deborah Jones and Gail Davis, two of his followers. Thinking that these women had tried to poison him, he made them disrobe at gunpoint and had them beaten. He forced a hot soldering iron into the mouth of one woman while the other had a toe squeezed in a vice. They were also forced to swallow detergent and another caustic liquid as part of their punishment. He was sentenced and served four years for the crime.[28]

A psychiatrist who examined Karenga noted that while in prison he had exhibited bizarre behavior, including talking to imaginary persons, claiming he was attacked by dive bombers, and claiming that his attorney was in the next cell with him. He was judged to be paranoid and schizophrenic.[29]

Karenga retired in 2002 as chair of the black studies department at Cal State, Long Beach, California. Professor Karenga had this cushy position for thirteen years where he used the cover of academic freedom to indoctrinate his students into Marxism, Afrocentrism, and hatred of America and whites.

Marxist Karenga's Kwanzaa celebration consists of seven principles, which are a blueprint for socialism, worship of false gods, and Afrocentrism. They are Umoja (unity), Kujichagulia (self-determination—

34

code, in this case, for Afrocentrism), Ujima (collective work and responsibility—groupthink), Ujamaa (cooperative economics—socialism), Nia (purpose), Kuumba (creativity), and Imani (faith—worship of false gods or no gods at all).

Karenga also created a Kwanzaa flag that consists of black, green, and red. The Kwanzaa Information Center describes the color red as representing blood: "We lost our land through blood; and we cannot gain it except through blood. We must redeem our lives through the blood. Without the shedding of blood there can be no redemption of this race." The Kwanzaa Information Center also notes that this flag "has become a symbol of devotion for African people in America to establish an independent African nation on the North American Continent."

Those who celebrate Kwanzaa are encouraged to pledge their allegiance to this flag. The pledge itself is a statement of racial hatred and black separatism:

> We pledge allegiance to the red, black, and green, our flag, the symbol of our eternal struggle, and to the land we must obtain; one nation of black people, with one God of us all, totally united in the struggle, for black love, black freedom, and black self-determination.[30]

Kwanzaa isn't a celebration of the African harvest; it is a political statement for the establishment of a separate black nation and racial hatred against whites.

When once asked why he designed Kwanzaa to take place around Christmas, Karenga explained, "People think it's African but it's not. I came up with Kwanzaa because Black people wouldn't celebrate it if they knew it was American. Also, I put it around Christmas because I knew that's when a lot of Bloods would be partying."[31]

Karenga has explained that his creation of Kwanzaa was motivated, in part, by hostility toward both Christianity and Judaism. Writing in his 1980 book *Kawaida Theory*, he claimed that Western religion "denies and diminishes human worth, capacity, potential and achievement. In Christian and Jewish mythology, humans are born in sin, cursed with mythical ancestors who've sinned and brought the wrath of an angry God on every generation's head." He clearly opposed belief in God and other "spooks who threaten us if we don't worship them and demand we turn over our destiny and daily lives."[32]

Unfortunately, Kwanzaa has been widely promoted in our culture, and even President George W. Bush issued a proclamation celebrating Kwanzaa in mid-December 2002.

Whites and blacks alike should tell the truth about Kwanzaa—but paralyzing fear keeps most whites from being willing to take a stand against what is clearly a subversive black nationalist movement designed to create racial separatism and hatred. Why should we be afraid of speaking out against a holiday invented by a Marxist hoodlum who tortures women and hates America?

THE KOOL-AID OF SOCIALISM

Black liberals and their white allies are in love with socialism, the welfare system, and centralized economic planning. Of course, they don't have the honesty to actually say they're socialists; they hide behind such words as "progressive" or "compassionate" to promote socialist policies.

Socialism is a destructive economic system that saps incentive, robs citizens of their hard-earned money, centralizes economic planning in the hands of a few liberal elitists, and creates a population that becomes indolent and dependent upon government handouts for its existence. This blind allegiance to social control and an economic system that doesn't work also continues to hold sway over black liberals in Congress.

The Congressional Black Caucus is a group of nearly forty legislators. Currently, eighteen of these liberals also belong to the Progressive Caucus, a group of nearly sixty legislators in the U.S. House of Representatives.

Joseph Farah, the founder and publisher of WorldNetDaily, has written extensively on the real purpose behind the Progressive Caucus. In a two-part series published on the WorldNetDaily web site in 1998,

Farah showed that the Progressive Caucus is simply a front group for the Democratic Socialists of America.

The Democratic Socialists of America web site openly describes its goal of working for socialism within the Democratic party. They encourage members to "stress our Democratic Party strategy and electoral work. The Democratic Party is something the public understands, and association with it takes the edge off. Stressing our Democratic Party work will establish some distance from the radical subculture and help integrate you to the milieu of the young liberals."

It is no surprise to me that nearly half of the members of the Black Caucus are also members of the Progressive Caucus because many black liberals are really just socialists in disguise. They want centralized control over our culture and economic life, they want government entitlement programs, and they can never have too many welfare programs to buy votes and to keep immoral blacks under their control.

The name of the game is control, and these characters are masters at keeping blacks on the Democratic party plantation. It matters little that socialism destroys while capitalism creates—as long as this socialistic system can keep people in bondage.

Blacks need to reject the anti-God, anti-capitalistic notions of these liberals and to pursue spiritual and material independence. Men and women must become their own leaders. I often say that you cannot ride two horses at one time. Blacks have to make a choice. When we make the commitment to know ourselves, we are laying the groundwork for true independence, which demagogues fear more than anything else.

3

Blacks Are *Not* Suffering Due to Racism

—⁓—

The lack of moral character is the number one problem in the black community today

If white Americans were to leave the country tomorrow, in ten years America would be a ghetto. You can see the truth of this when you look at many of our major cities that are run by black mayors, black-dominated city councils, and black police chiefs. These cities are usually horrible places to live. Yet blacks who live in black-ruled cities can't see the truth: their own immorality is the cause of black poverty, crime, and family destruction!

But liberal black leaders have so successfully brainwashed most black Americans about the topic of "racism" that it has created what seems to be an alternate reality among blacks. Not only is there paranoia about AIDS and crack cocaine being "white man" plots, but also blacks see racism everywhere they look, even though by most accounts there is really very little racism left among whites—certainly not among those with much power and influence.

The sad truth is that black racism is far more pervasive today than is white racism. These negative attitudes affect blacks and their ability to function in our multiracial culture. Polls and surveys indicate that blacks have a skewed view of the truth when it comes to racism against blacks—and even about racism against other minority groups. A Gallup Poll conducted in 2001 revealed this pessimism. A majority of blacks polled—66 percent—believe that race will always be a problem in America, while only 45 percent of whites agreed.[1]

Whites are more hopeful that racial harmony can exist between blacks and whites, yet most blacks have been so conditioned by the problem profiteers that their paranoia hinders their ability to judge each person by his character and not by the color of his skin.

Black racism against whites is pervasive and has no sign of abating as long as blacks blindly follow their Jim Jones "civil rights" leaders. These leaders must keep racial tensions high and must constantly look for new signs of "white racism" in order to justify their existence. If they ever did actually solve these alleged problems of racism between whites and blacks, they'd be out of business.

IT'S NOT RACISM—IT'S LACK OF CHARACTER

I have been working with troubled black boys from the inner cities and from broken homes in my organization since 1990. Out of the hundreds of cases I've been involved in, white racism had nothing to do with any of the problems these kids have.

These kids have anger, emotional, drug, and authority problems because they come from broken homes or homes that have been filled with violence. They have come from homes without a father and with a mother who is often angry at *all* men because she was abandoned by *her* man. These boys have gotten into trouble with the law because they're angry at their absentee or weak dads, and they're in rebellion against their mothers for being overbearing or abusive. They join gangs in order to have a "family," and they start selling drugs because it's a quick way out of poverty. They think selling drugs and acting like a "gangsta" is cool. This "thug life" was made popular by the late rapper Tupac Shakur, who was shot to death in Las Vegas in September of 1996. So many other young black men have tragically met similar fates while trying to live the "thug life."

Of course, this turns out to be a dead-end street for them. Once they start selling drugs they must protect their territory, and this inevitably leads to gun violence and frequently to death. There are other ugly by-products of this lifestyle, such as incarceration and promiscuous sex, which often leads to sexually transmitted diseases, including AIDS.

These kids have never learned a proper work ethic or patience, nor have they seen good role models, which by the way, are far more powerful than words. Too many parents tell their kids one thing and do another. This is incredibly damaging.

These kids grow up lazy, angry, and prone to violence because they live in an environment that is more like a jungle than a civilized community. These kids drop out of school and spend their time listening to gangsta rap music that teaches them to hate police and all authority, to treat women like whores, and to look at guns and drugs as their way out of poverty. The music they listen to becomes their tutor—and the corruption that results is plain for all to see.

And although we would like to believe that only poor blacks are subject to this lifestyle and its inherent curses, selling drugs is common even among middle class and affluent black males who grow up in single-parent or effectively single-parent homes.

The absence of the father creates a hole in the center of their being, particularly for boys. Their lives become a routine of "looking for love in all the wrong places," as the song says. When a young black male cannot find love at home, he hits the streets and seeks acceptance from other young men. These boys crave the respect and acceptance they get (or perceive they get) from their peers when they sell drugs.

We have a generation of kids who have no character, no moral base to live by, and no real hope for the future. The prisons are filled with these kids and more are on their way because of the destruction of the black family and the lack of moral leadership within churches and from black leaders.

LAZY AND IRRESPONSIBLE

This isn't a politically correct position to have, but I'm convinced that the lack of moral character in many black men is the primary cause of the breakdown of the black family, high crime rates, domestic violence, and other social problems within the black community.

From working with black males for more than a dozen years, I can say with confidence that many black males are both lazy and irresponsible. This view isn't popular with problem profiteers who blame all black woes upon white racism or poverty, but it is true, nonetheless.

The young men I work with represent just the tip of the iceberg of a far larger laziness problem within the black male population. The typical black male I work with has no work ethic, has little sense of direction in his life, is hostile toward whites and women, has an attitude of entitlement, and has an amoral outlook on life.

He has no strong male role model in his life to teach him the value of hard work, patience, self-control, and character. He is emotionally adrift and is nearly illiterate—either because he dropped out of school or because he's just not motivated enough to learn.

Many of the black males I've worked with have had a "don't give a damn" attitude toward work and life and believe that "white America" owes them a living. They have no shame about going on welfare because they believe whites owe them for past discrimination and slavery. This absurd thinking results in a lifetime of laziness and blaming, while taxpayers pick up the tab for individuals who lack character and a strong work ethic.

Frequently, blacks who attempt to enter the workforce often become problems for their employers. This is because they also have an entitlement mentality that puts little emphasis on working hard to get ahead. They expect to be paid for doing little work, often show up late, and have bad attitudes while on the job. They're so sensitized to "racism" that they feel abused by every slight, no matter if it's intentional, unconscious, or even based in reality.

Employers are nervous about how they should treat their black employees. They understandably fear EEOC lawsuits or civil rights complaints, regardless of whether these result from real or imagined slights. Many employers rightfully consider a black employee a walking time bomb. A racist black who goes to work for a corporation poses a daily threat to the leaders of the business because all he needs do is make a phone call to Jesse Jackson and all hell will break loose for that company. Jackson will march into town with his racist minions, and the negative publicity they generate will result in millions of dollars in losses to the corporation.

If employed blacks maintain a hostile attitude toward their employers and their fellow workers, they will inevitably be passed over for promotions and thus will cry "racism" as the cause of their lack of upward mobility. The cycle of self-destruction continues, and no one wins except the civil rights leaders who can then extract millions from fearful corporate leaders.

SEXUAL IMMORALITY FUELS AIDS EPIDEMIC

Sexual immorality in the black community is totally out of control. This has resulted not only in an epidemic of sexually transmitted diseases such as syphilis but also a growing AIDS epidemic. This is being fueled by a militant homosexual movement that is now focusing its attention on recruitment within the black community.

As more blacks start engaging in homosexual conduct, we will see a continued spread of AIDS into the community. Many of these individuals engage in bisexual activities, so they're not only infecting each other but also infecting women.

The statistics are depressing and will worsen with time. According to recent Centers for Disease Control (CDC) statistics, of the estimated forty thousand new HIV infections each year, more than 50 percent occur among black Americans.

- In 1998, black women constituted 64 percent of new female AIDS cases, and black men accounted for 50 percent of new AIDS cases.

- AIDS is the number one cause of death for black adults aged 25 to 44, before heart disease, cancer, and homicide.

- One in 50 black men is HIV-positive. One in 160 black women is HIV-positive.

- Black senior citizens represent more than 50 percent of HIV cases among persons over age 55.

- Intravenous drug use is fueling the epidemic in black communities. It accounts for 43 percent of infections among black women and 38 percent among black men. Many women contract HIV through sex with an intravenous drug user.

- In 1998, men of color who have sex with men represented 52 percent of total AIDS cases. By comparison, in 1989, men of color who have sex with men represented 31 percent of total AIDS cases.

- Although only 15 percent of the adolescent population in the United States is black, over 60 percent of AIDS cases reported in 1999 among 13-19 year olds were among blacks.

- Black children represent almost two-thirds (62 percent) of all reported pediatric AIDS cases.[2]

And what is the proposed solution by liberal blacks to this horrendous challenge facing blacks? It's not to discourage homosexual sex or to teach abstinence. No, the new mantra of those who are supposedly going to fight AIDS within the black community is "stigma."

A liberal group known as The Balm in Gilead has seized a leadership role in the AIDS crisis within the black community, and it has directed its energies toward establishing AIDS programs within churches. This group, headed by Pernessa Seele, has received funding from the Ford Foundation and the CDC. Seele is an advisor to the leftist Congressional Black Caucus, so her message to the churches is predictable: the "stigma" against homosexuality and sexuality in general in churches has helped create the AIDS crisis within the black community.

Seele recommends programs in black churches designed to remove this "stigma" from homosexuality, and she has urged that condoms be freely distributed as a way of helping fight AIDS.

In effect, Seele's group is using the AIDS crisis within the black community to promote tolerance for homosexuality and for the distribution of condoms. These "solutions" will only worsen the problem. Her solution will increase the numbers of homosexuals in black communities, result in more AIDS infections, and create an environment where immoral sexual activities are validated—as long as one uses a condom.

One of Seele's latest activities involves a "Black Church Week of Prayer for the Healing of AIDS," with more than five thousand black churches participating.[3] What are these pastors thinking? Will the promotion of homosexual sex stop the spread of AIDS? Will the distribution of condoms stop AIDS? Homosexual sex is what spread AIDS in the first place, and condoms will never provide complete protection from AIDS or any other sexually transmitted disease.

These pastors should be teaching morality and sexual abstinence, and they should be preaching powerful sermons against homosexuality! Instead, these blind pastors are following corrupt liberals whose foolish policies will only increase the number of deaths within black communities.

Public schools are teaching both white and black children that homosexual sex is normal and that they should be free to choose whatever sexual partners they wish to have. As a result, more and more boys and girls—including black boys and girls—are experimenting with homosexual behavior.

There are spiritual laws in effect that blacks cannot break without severe consequences. One of these is sexual abstinence before marriage and fidelity in marriage. By promoting homosexuality and condom distribution programs, these pastors are violating spiritual truths and condemning members of their congregations to certain death. These are blind leaders of the blind.

When young people violate these spiritual laws, they become less subject to God in their lives and become more and more enslaved to other people—or even to sexual activity. This bondage leads inevitably to unwanted pregnancies, venereal diseases, abortion, and even death from AIDS. A person cannot expect to violate spiritual laws without serious personal and social consequences.

ABORTION AND ILLEGITIMACY RATES REMAIN HIGH

From my work with young black men, I have found that premarital sex is on the rise and the age at which a child engages in sex is becoming lower and lower. Some young black girls are now starting to have sex at the age of nine or ten.

Black women are acting irresponsibly by giving birth to baby after baby out of wedlock. Most of these children are from different fathers as well. These irresponsible men simply roam like wild beasts in heat from one woman to another and impregnate as many as possible without regard for the women or their children, dodging accountability as they go. These foolish women allow themselves to be used by these sexual predators and continue to give birth to babies who grow up without fathers. And, with fathers ducking responsibility, the welfare system picks up the tab for a big percentage of these illegitimate children.

The irresponsibility of black men and women is creating a cycle of poverty, mental disorders, and violence within the black community. This is not the result of white racism but immorality and the lack of character! I hold black men primarily responsible for this mess because they're supposed to be the leaders in the home. There is a divine order to family life, and it's one that can't be violated without severe consequences. That order is God in Christ, Christ in man, man over woman, and woman over children. The man is to function as the president of his family; his wife is the vice president. Yet black men have fled from this responsibility, and the results are there for all to see!

In addition to illegitimacy and fatherlessness, abortion rates are extremely high in the black community. According to Peggy Lehner, president of the Right to Life Committee in Dayton, Ohio, "In 1997, the most recent year for which national statistics are available, 35.9 percent of all abortions were performed on African-American women. This percentage has continued to increase virtually every year since 1973, when African-American abortions represented just 23 percent of all abortions."[4]

Since 1973, when abortion was legalized in the United States, more than 13 million black babies have been killed in abortion clinics. Abortion is now one of the leading causes of death in the black community.

Lehner points out an interesting fact about the relationship of abortion to church attendance among black women. She writes:

One of the few in-depth sociological studies we found related to this issue noted that while in the 1970s church attendance was a contributing factor toward an African-American woman's opposition to abortion, by the 90s this factor had disappeared. It is our theory that as the abortion issue became a dogma of the Democratic Party, the Black Church, which has been intimately linked to the party, grew silent. This could account for the muddy theology we hear so frequently expressed on the issue.

Many of the women we talked with expressed strong religious opposition to abortion. However, they also believed that God readily forgives abortion, since God knows the personal circumstances that would make abortion a woman's "only" option.[5]

This is a serious indictment of the Black Church, and I'm convinced that it is accurate. The Black Church has largely become a tool of the Democratic party, and it adheres to the party line on every issue—including the intentional killing of an unborn child through abortion. But it is not "muddy theology" that comes forth from black pastors. It is evil. Instead of standing for the sanctity of life and marriage, too many black pastors have retreated into silence and promote a political platform as more important than the ethical standards of the Bible.

BLACK CRIME IS OUT OF CONTROL

In Los Angeles in 2002, there were an estimated 600 murders—and a large number of these were blacks killing blacks. Black-on-black crime is a growing national problem, but this is only one part of the overall scandal of black crime in our nation.

Recent FBI statistics show that blacks commit half of all homicides, nearly half of all rapes, 59 percent of robberies, and 38 percent of aggravated assaults. Dr. Walter E. Williams rightly says that these high crime rates aren't the result of poverty or discrimination. These rates "represent political choices made by black politicians, civil rights organizations and many black citizens who tolerate criminals." [6]

Liberals can complain all they want about racism in the justice system, institutional racism, disparate sentencing for drug offenses, etc., but the truth of the matter is that young black males simply commit far more crimes of violence than do whites or other minority groups. The statistics are undeniably accurate. Claiming that racism is the cause of black crime rates is absurd and shifts the blame away from the real culprits: the violent young men who turn to crime to satisfy their lust for guns, power, money, control, and women.

Crime will continue to rise within our inner cities because police have decided to avoid many of these high crime areas in order to avoid being called racists for enforcing the law. This phenomenon has been building for years but has become more obvious since the rioting that occurred in Cincinnati, Ohio, in 2001. The melee was prompted when a white policeman killed an unarmed black youth. According to black activist Robert Woodson, police in Cincinnati have decided to "de-police" the more dangerous areas of the city in order to avoid being labeled racists. As a result of this de-policing policy in Cincinnati, there's been an 800 percent increase in violence in those areas. [7] Gang activity in numerous major cities is on the rise as well because police fear having their careers destroyed by being called racists when they attempt to arrest criminals.

Thanks to the combined efforts of black racists and black criminals who cry "racism" and "police brutality" whenever police enforce the law, the inner cities are going to become more dangerous and chaotic. Police are criticized when they don't go after criminals in black neighborhoods, but they know that if they vigorously enforce the law, they will be arresting blacks and will open themselves up to charges of racism. Police are caught in a no-win situation. By de-policing, they protect themselves, but the real victims of the race scammers are the decent blacks who simply want to live in peace.

Worse, while often complaining of crime, black leaders do not do enough to denounce the criminals themselves. No better example exists for this failure than that of Maxine Waters, who became the target of syndicated columnist Michele Malkin in 2000 for this very reason:

> This is a woman who excused the 1992 Los Angeles riots as a "rebellion." This is a woman who called the violence in Los Angeles, "a spontaneous reaction to a lot of injustice and a lot of alienation and frustration." This is a woman who, instead of coming to the aid of Korean grocers and other minority business owners in her district whose lives were destroyed by looters, made statements such as this:
>
> "There were mothers who took this as an opportunity to take some milk, to take some bread, to take some shoes. Maybe they shouldn't have done it, but the atmosphere was such that they did it. They are not crooks." And this: "One lady said her children didn't have any shoes. She just saw those shoes there, a chance for all of her children to have new shoes. . . . It was such a tear-jerker. I might have gone in and taken them for her myself."
>
> This is a woman who danced the electric slide with Crips and Bloods gang members and then noted in her official biography: 'Many young people, including those in the hip-hop music community, praise her for her fearless support and understanding of young people and their efforts at self-expression.'[8]

Maxine Waters gave aid and comfort to the looters and the killers who rampaged through Los Angeles after the Rodney King trial. Instead of condemning these criminals for shooting and trying to beat to death innocent bystanders—and for burning down hundreds of Korean businesses—Waters justifies this kind of lawless activity and even suggests she might have joined in the looting. This, from a woman who sits in the U.S. Congress, makes our laws, and is reelected year after year by blacks in Los Angeles!

CLASHING WITH DANNY GLOVER

Film star Danny Glover is well known for his role as a tough police detective in the *Lethal Weapon* series with Mel Gibson. But he's far less known by most Americans for his radical views about America. Glover has been involved in a variety of extreme leftist causes, including anti-death penalty campaigns and international conferences on racism, and he currently opposes our nation's war on terrorism.

Glover was a speaker at an Amnesty International anti-death penalty seminar held at Princeton University on November 15, 2001. Glover figured he was in friendly territory, so he could rant about President Bush and our nation's supposedly racist judicial system. He was wrong. In the audience was a young BOND member, Scott Stewart.

Glover was about to have an encounter with a young man who refused to be intimidated or shouted into submission. During his speech, Glover told the audience that President Bush had built his career on "the backs of death row inmates," and he complained bitterly that 43 percent of the prisoners on death row were blacks while blacks only make up 12.1 percent of the total population.

During the Q&A session, Stewart got up and said, "Mr. Glover, you correctly pointed out that blacks are disproportionately victims of the death penalty. What you failed to mention, however, is that in 1999 blacks committed seven times the homicides than did whites. Also, in the twenty-four years prior to that, blacks committed at least five times the murders whites did. You act as if this racial disproportion comes out of nowhere, like it's some sort of accident."[9]

At this point, a number of people in the audience started hissing at

Stewart. As the crowd got louder, Glover tried to act as a mediator to calm them down. Stewart continued, "As the recipient of an NAACP Image Award, you have been endorsed by the largest civil rights organization in the country to be a sort of hero to the black community, to be someone that is looked up to. I think it's a tragedy that you act as if this whole problem is some sort of random racial disparity rather than addressing the real problems in the black community, such as fatherlessness."

Glover began to answer Stewart by belittling him, "Well, you're obviously very young," and then claimed that, "White cops are shooting blacks all the time." Stewart yelled back, "A black cop is twice as likely to shoot a black suspect than is a white cop!"

Glover then lost it and launched into a tirade about blacks as victims of a racist America. He told Stewart, "When you're fifty-five-years old like I am, you'll probably still have no clue. I'm a fifty-five-year old—" Stewart cut him off mid-sentence: "A fifty-five-year-old professional victim!"

Glover, who already had smoke coming out of his ears, looked at Stewart and said, "What did you say!?" Stewart reiterated, "A fifty-five-year-old professional victim!" Pandemonium ensued.

Danny Glover's encounter with Scott Stewart revealed the truth about this actor and his black racist beliefs. It also showed how really ignorant he was of the facts, which probably explains why he remains a darling of the Hate America and black racist crowd.

"GANGSTA" RAP MUSIC CREATES
ANTISOCIAL ATTITUDES

Advertisers spend billions of dollars a year to influence the opinions, tastes, and philosophies of their potential customers. Advertisers know they can get people to buy their products by producing a constant bombardment of images, words, and music through TV, radio, print advertising, the Internet, and other media outlets.

Rap music executives and rap musicians are also selling a product, but many are selling more than just music. They're selling an ideology, a way of life, and an attitude with their lyrics and visual images.

Russell Simmons, the co-founder of Def Jam Records, is an occasional guest on the Fox News show "The O'Reilly Factor." When challenged by Bill O'Reilly to justify the profanity, hate, and sexual violence in rap music, Simmons's typical response is that rap music is a cry for help or a mirror of the reality of growing up in a ghetto.

In an interview with Simmons on December 13, 2002, O'Reilly discussed the appointment of Def Jam Records rapper Jay-Z to become an honorary principal in twelve public high schools throughout the United States. Bill O'Reilly asked Simmons why there couldn't be a better role model for students. Here's Simmons's reply: "Well, first, you have to understand rap is a voice of a lot of voiceless people. You may hear some poverty and ignorance in their voice, but then that's their reality, in some cases, and that reality, that truth, I think, is very relevant and important."[10]

Jay-Z is nothing more than a street hoodlum who has become a millionaire—thanks to Russell Simmons and other rap music moguls. Jay-Z was charged with the stabbing of a fellow rap music associate, Lance Rivera, in December of 1999 at a New York nightclub. He was also charged a month earlier with smashing a bottle over the head of a man at the same sleazy night club. Jay-Z received three years probation for the stabbing incident and continues to make millions from his obscene music.

In one song, "Murdergram," he says he will "spit with murderous intentions" anyone who challenges him and threatens to "put you six feet deep."

In "Money, Cash, Hoes," Jay-Z, the honorary principal of twelve high schools, says: "Money cash hoes money cash chicks what / Sex murder and mayhem romance for the street / Only wife of mines is a life of crime."

This man is hardly a proper role model for high school students or black teens who listen to rap music, yet these antisocial messages are repeatedly pounded into the heads of young people—both white and black.

Rapper Dr. Dre's music is just as obscene and antisocial. His themes involve promoting hatred and disrespect for women and hatred of the police. Dr. Dre was co-founder of NWA, an acronym for "Niggaz with Attitude." One of NWA's most notable songs was "F—- tha Police."

Then there's the very popular 50 Cent, whom Dr. Dre and Eminem produce. 50 Cent has been heavily hyped by Eminem, the popular white rapper. Supposedly 50 Cent is the "real deal"—he came from the worst neighborhoods, has been shot, etc. Here's a sample of his "artistry": "Come off, now watch your chain / Fo' I blow out your brains. . . . When witnesses around, they know how we get down / So when the cops come they ain't seen s—- mayn."

Of course, there's also Snoop Dogg, a rapper who gained fame with Death Row Records. In 2001, Snoop Dogg teamed up with *Hustler* magazine publisher Larry Flynt to produce a pornographic music video called "Doggystyle," described as a cross between a rap video and an XXX-rated movie. He also has an album by the same name. Snoop Dogg went out on his own in 2002 and began producing his own pornographic videos called "Girls Gone Wild: Doggy Style." The first in the series of these videos shows Snoop Dogg at Mardi Gras persuading hundreds of drunken girls to expose themselves to the camera.

Given Jay-Z's qualifications, Snoop's immoral and violence-filled music (not to mention his new foray into the production of pornography) makes him a logical candidate to become the next honorary principal at a high school near you.

While Russell Simmons claims that rap music is just expressing a reality that needs to be heard, the truth of the matter is that many rap artists are simply thugs who promote violence, rebellion against authority, disrespect for women, hatred of whites, the use of gutter language, and the glorification of drug use.

This ideology of hatred and violence is precisely the wrong message for black teenagers to be hearing. Bill O'Reilly, in a column for WorldNetDaily, described the ultimate consequences of gangsta rap music on impressionable black kids:

What about those black kids trapped in ghettos with little parental supervision and guidance? Are rap themes going to help them get out of their dire circumstance?

The answer is no. If those kids adopt vulgarity in their speech, an anti-white attitude, and an acceptance of dope and violence, the only way they're likely to leave the hood is on a stretcher or in the back of a police cruiser. Hard work and discipline punch the ticket out of poverty. Thinking up rhymes about cocaine is not going to go far on a college admissions application.[11]

I believe that this type of rap music is ultimately one of the most dangerous and destructive forces within the black community. Rap music is often more important to most black teens than school attendance. In effect, the ideas in rap music become the dominant worldview of teens—their religious view of the world—and these ideas are destroying any sense of morality, decency, racial harmony, or respect for authority in teens.

Rap music elevates the most degrading vices into virtues and encourages a lifestyle that can only be described as depraved. Once these ideas are imbedded in the minds of teens, they produce a lifestyle of self-sabotage and lead to the destruction of all those around them. The young person who guides his life by the gutter philosophies of rap artists is doomed to failure—and it is likely he will take others down with him.

IT'S CHARACTER, STUPID!

Blacks who have adopted a welfare mentality, a racist worldview, and a Snoop Dogg morality can expect to fail in this life. This corruption of character should be condemned by black churches, civil rights leaders, and black congressmen, but it won't be. These are the negative and destructive attitudes that these leaders *want* blacks to have so they can continue profiting from their lucrative "black as victim" industry.

What blacks should be doing is pursuing character, learning how to support themselves through honest work, and letting go of hatred, blame, and racism. Only then will blacks truly see a radical change within their communities and their lives.

Where does this process of healing begin? It must begin in the hearts and minds of black men and women—but I am especially concerned that it begin in black men. They are the key. They must reject racism, embrace personal responsibility, become good fathers and husbands, and learn the value of hard work. They must be faithful in marriage, train their children to love what is right, and become model employees or employers. They must also reject the phony agendas and ideas of the dangerous con men who exploit them to build their own wealth and power.

4

A Church and Liquor Store
on Every Corner

—◊—

*Too often the intent of church leaders
is to control, not to set people free*

I t seems as though everybody and their mama attends church in the black community. This is because the church remains a powerful institution in black communities—much more so than in many white communities.

The trouble is, while most blacks talk about God and attend church, far too many are living lives that are morally bankrupt and hypocritical. They may say they believe in God, but they don't let Him control their lives. They know about Him, but they have never developed a personal relationship with Him.

There's a lot of "soul" in black churches, but very little evidence of the Holy Spirit. You know what I'm talking about: You can see choirs clapping and singing loudly on televised church services, and you can see the pastor strutting back and forth across the stage wiping his brow with a face cloth. He may be screaming at the top of his lungs, but there's little depth to his message. It's just emotional hype and doesn't do a thing to truly change lives.

To do that, black pastors must step up and encourage parishioners to straighten out their lives, but they seldom rebuke or correct the sinful behaviors of their congregants. If you attend a typical black church today, you'll think you're attending a financial planning seminar or a Tony Robbins-style motivational speech. You'll get a self-help pep talk and hear plenty of sermons on how to get rich—and how to make the pastor rich—but you'll hear very little about how to be truly free. That's the sad state of the black church today, and I don't see things getting much better unless blacks have a complete change of heart.

CORRUPTION JUNCTION

The black church has been thoroughly compromised by Democratic politics and the radical agendas of homosexuals and Afrocentrists who preach anti-white racism.

One example of this corruption is the Faith United Methodist Church in Los Angeles, headed by Rev. M. Andrew Robinson-Gaither. During the Christmas holiday of 2001, Robinson-Gaither and his church members went on a seven-day fast to celebrate Kwanzaa as a way of focusing on the church's food pantry for those suffering from AIDS. In doing so, he acted as an enabler for homosexuals, who are dying from perverted sex, while muting the only real saving power by diluting the celebration of Christ's birth with Ron Karenga's phony racist holiday.

Gaither claims that the black church must "stop criticizing and condemning and singling out homosexuality." He says the church is less likely to condemn "men and women who have illegitimate babies. . . . Why do we do it to same-gender-loving couples?"[1]

When I first heard about Robinson-Gaither's antics, I was outraged. Interviewed by the *Los Angeles Times* about these activities, I told the reporter, "Jesus did not hand out condoms. . . . We've got to overcome sin, not mask an inner death. [Homosexuals are] dying spiritually, and all you're doing is preserving the physical just a little longer." I told the reporter that this is stern but sound theology. "If it takes people dying to change their ways, then let them die."[2]

I know that sounds harsh, but what is worse: accepting homosexual behavior into the church so that more people will die of AIDS or taking a stand against dangerous and immoral sexual practices? Robinson-Gaither will have more AIDS deaths on his hands by accepting homosexuality as normal behavior. This is hardly a loving response. You don't approve of sin as a way of dealing with sin—and you don't redefine sin to suit your personal opinions.

Gaither, of course, is blinded by his leftist and racist ideology. The *Los Angeles Times* article revealed that Faith United has long been a hotbed of radical leftist activities and Afrocentric racism. Robinson-Gaither's church was where the "LA-4" met to plan their legal defense after the Rodney King riots in 1992. The LA-4 was the group of four black thugs who pulled the white truck driver Reginald Denny from his truck, kicked him nearly to death, and smashed his head with a brick. Live news footage of this beating showed one of the hoodlums, Damien "Football" Williams, dancing around Denny's bloodied body.

Gaither's so-called church was also where former Black Panther leader Geronimo Pratt visited first after he was released from prison. Pratt had been sent to prison in 1968 for the robbery and murder of a school teacher. He was released from prison in 1997 on what some believe to be a technicality.

What kind of "church" is this? It appears to operate more like a communist front group than a church that honors God. One can only wonder what kind of spiritual food Robinson-Gaither's members receive each week from a man who speaks approvingly of sodomy, helps defend black rioters, and provides a welcome home to radical, violent leftists and Afrocentric racists.

Gaither's alleged "church" is a sad and disgusting example of what passes for black Christianity today.

I frequently have black pastors on my radio show because I want to confront them about their hidden racist views and their leftist political ideas. I also confront them about immorality in the church. The slogan we use on our show is "Revealing the lie so that you can see the truth." There are four typical responses I get on my show from preachers: 1) they talk around a question unceasingly, no matter how many times I attempt to get them to answer directly with simple language; 2) they quote the Bible with no additional conversation to elucidate the text or explain its meaning; 3) they call me names; or 4) they hang up. Actually, you'd be surprised how often we get the last response. Very seldom do we actually get an honest preacher who either admits what he does not know or demonstrates an understanding of what he preaches.

I invited Robinson-Gaither on my radio show once to discuss his political agenda, but he couldn't take the heat and hung up on me. I merely shrugged and added him to my show's ever-growing "Coward's List." (I urge you to check "The Jesse Lee Peterson Radio Show" archives on our web site at www.BondInfo.org to hear a number of these interesting confrontations.)

CALLED BY MAMA

One of the reasons people like Robinson-Gaither have the power and influence they do is that churchgoing is an ingrained habit in the black community. We grow up going to church—it's just part of the culture.

As men have drifted more and more into irresponsibility, women have typically been the driving force behind getting them to go to church. Realizing this, pastors tend to pander to women; they know who their core audience is. Many black men see these ministers as money-hungry hypocrites. Why would they then they continue to attend and support such men? Forced to go to church by their mothers and grandmothers, as they have grown older, these men have simply developed a habit of churchgoing.

The same is even true for many of these pastors. Most black ministers are not called by God—they're called by their mamas. Oftentimes, a young black boy will say something that sounds intelligent, and his mother or grandmother will say, "Boy, one day you're gonna be a preacher!" So he becomes a preacher. He doesn't really have what it takes to lead people; all he can do is pander and flatter his flock.

For these pastors, as for their followers, churchgoing is a cultural thing, not a spiritual thing. The average minister has a great desire for power and wealth. He understands how conditioned blacks have become to churchgoing, so he tells his followers God "called" him to set up a church. It's the magic phrase. No matter what the lifestyle of the minister is, blacks typically will continue to support him. It's just what a person is supposed to do. (In fact, the ingrained, unquestioning support for the civil rights establishment has its origins in the unwavering support blacks have for pastors—usually the first black leaders we ever meet in life.)

These pastors have often been responsible for leading their congregations astray. Instead of looking to God, they are taught to look to other gods—the god of government programs or the god of the so-called black leader. This puts most blacks right in the pocket of the Democratic party, which has become a god for many as well.

TENDING THE DEMOCRATIC PLANTATION

I often speak in churches about the need for blacks to become free of their Democratic party exploiters and their leftist agendas. But this isn't a popular topic. Pastors don't want to hear this message, and their congregations have been so brainwashed by liberal propaganda that they become outraged at me for telling them the truth.

The corruption of the black church by radical liberalism is clearly evident in the slavish loyalty that black pastors and blacks in general give to former President Bill Clinton. Even though this evil man was thoroughly exposed as a liar, adulterer, and sexual pervert, and despite the fact that he was guilty of near-treasonous activity in allowing nuclear technology to be transferred to China, black pastors still invited him into their churches so he could spew out his lies.

The Rev. John Cherry of Full Gospel AME Zion Church in Temple Hills, Maryland, for example, invited Clinton to speak in his church in 1995, to lobby for passage of a crime bill. Cherry could hardly have been ignorant of Clinton's support of homosexuality, abortion, socialism, and other anti-God policies, yet because of blind loyalty to the Democratic party, this pastor allowed this corrupt man to infect his church with lies.

The continued loyalty that black "Christians" have to Clinton is disgusting in light of all that is known about this man's despicable behavior toward women, unborn babies, and the truth. In fact, their unquestioning loyalty to Clinton is still so absolute that the Black Hall of Fame in Little Rock, Arkansas, actually inducted Clinton—the first white person ever to be so honored.

The Black Hall of Fame founder Charles Stewart gushed over Clinton with these words: "It is this community's way of saying thank you to him for the work that he has done."[3]

Other honorees in the Black Hall of Fame include former U.S. Surgeon General Joycelyn Elders and the pretentious poet Maya Angelou, who read her rambling verses at President Clinton's first inauguration. Elders, of course, has recommended teaching kids how to masturbate as part of the high school sex education curriculum. She now lobbies for the legalization of prostitution. Clinton is in good company with the likes of Elders.

The strange loyalty that black liberals have to Clinton is mind-boggling and shows the extent to which blacks—even black pastors—have been seduced by this man's demonic charm. Writer Toni Morrison claimed several years ago that Clinton was America's first "black" president. What does this mean? I guess it means that to be truly "black" one must be a committed serial adulterer, liar, pervert, and socialist. You're apparently not "black" if you support morality, capitalism, and faithfulness in marriage.

Charles Stewart has sent a horrible message to blacks by inducting Clinton into the Black Hall of Fame. Clinton should have been removed from office and jailed for his various crimes, but he has escaped the justice he so richly deserves. He is hardly a role model for blacks.

While Clinton was president, polls consistently showed that approximately 90 percent of black Americans supported him. This is after he admitted to having an "inappropriate relationship" with Monica Lewinsky (and that only after lying to the American people and his cabinet for seven months by saying that he did not have this relationship). It was also after Kenneth Starr's report was released and after the public got a videotaped look at the president's slippery, absurd testimony, where he invented new definitions for words like "alone" and "is."

After reading the Starr report for myself, I discovered that the president, the chief law enforcement officer in this country, had clearly lied under oath. Knowing that the black community had also seen the report but had chosen to go into denial regarding its ugly contents, my initial reaction was one of sadness. I was saddened because I realized how low the black community as a whole has fallen morally, to the point of being nearly devoid of any values or character. I also realized how the love of God and country has become almost extinct in the black community.

Seeing the black reaction to Kenneth Starr's report also caused me to see, more clearly than ever, how effective the brainwashing by Jesse Jackson, Maxine Waters, the NAACP, Al Sharpton, Louis Farrakhan, and the Black Caucus truly is. *But they couldn't have done it alone.* These leaders needed men in the pulpit regularly defending Clinton, men who could piously intone about the need to love and forgive—despite the fact that the president exhibited no sign of concern for his wrongs.

The call to forgive Clinton's antics despite his lack of repentance is a glaring example of the problem of sin in black churches. Sexual sin is often dismissed or swept under the rug, be it homosexuality, promiscuity, or adultery. My God instructs me to forgive; that much is true. And pastors *should* encourage forgiveness. But God also causes us to pay a price for our sin. What we put out comes back to us. This is a spiritual law, created by God. By not standing against sin, pastors have become enablers of it, and these sorts of sins are the kinds that destroy communities.

FORGIVE AND FORGET?

I have often heard blacks say that we are the most forgiving race of people. The usual example to prove this claim is that we have forgiven slavery, etc. But let me be plain: blacks are not forgiving. We would not have spent the last forty years complaining, whimpering, whining, and begging if we were forgiving. We would not be accusing whites of being racists and of trying to hold us back if we were truly forgiving. Forgiving people have clarity of vision. We would see that Bill Clinton used us by throwing us bones (welfare, affirmative action) for his own personal gain. The former president has carefully culti-vated black favor because he knows it forms an important part of his support.

To show blacks how much he empathized with them, Clinton formed a race panel, apologized to Africa for American slavery, wel-comed communist Nelson Mandela to the U.S. as a hero, and, after his presidency, set up offices in Harlem—among other phony gestures.

A discerning mind could see that Bill Clinton's overtures to blacks have not only been an embarrassment, they have been actually harm-ful. For instance, as president, he offered blacks the public school sys-tem, yet sent his daughter to the best private school. It is also said that Bill Clinton was the first president to put blacks in high positions in his administration. This may have been true, but look at the kind of black people he put there—mainly those as morally bankrupt as he (Joycelyn Elders, etc.). It became clear that most blacks preferred programs over principles. They preferred cheap, empty, and even injurious gestures over real presidential leadership. Where's the shame?

Many blacks asked for forgiveness for the president, but they typi-cally misrepresented the word. They really didn't believe an offense had been committed in the first place. They simply wanted others to move on because they already had.

Dr. Martin Luther King's daughter used the Bible to support her brand of forgiveness for President Clinton. She said, "God forgave King David for his sins."[4] But what she forgot to point out was that, yes, God forgave King David, but the king still paid a price. He didn't just go on with business as usual. Shame on Miss King, daughter of such a great man, and a so-called "woman of God." In reality she is a supporter of sin. How could Dr. King have left behind a daughter so ignorant?

Today the black church is not a place where one goes to overcome sin, but rather to deny its very existence. Many examples in my own city abound: Rev. Robinson-Gaither defending homosexuality, Rev. Cecil Murray at First AME Church distributing condoms, Bishop Charles Blake at West Angeles Church of God in Christ allowing black politicians to come into his church and encouraging hatred toward whites. None of these preachers (all supposedly called by God) has ever, to my knowledge, rebuked the others or Bill Clinton—at least not publicly.

Forty years ago, blacks were ashamed of sin. If a woman found herself pregnant without a husband, she generally kept it secret for fear of destroying the family name. Her father would sometimes talk to the man and convince him to do the right thing and marry his daughter. If a preacher committed adultery, he would not only be forced out of his church, but the community as well. Sex out of wedlock, particularly by young people, was hidden from adults out of fear of punishment and a high respect for elders. Lying to parents, teachers, or preachers was unheard of. If it did occur, punishment was swift and sure.

Forty years ago, when the racially discriminatory Jim Crow laws were in place, sex before marriage was rare and abortion rates were low. Personal morality and family togetherness were prized. Love of parents was real, hard work was the norm, and men were strong. The current pathetic state of morality in the black community is a slap in the face to those blacks who suffered and died for our freedom. Prior to forty years ago, blacks were physically handicapped by the laws but mentally and morally stout.

God is giving all Americans, particularly blacks, a chance to look at themselves and to rise to a higher standard of morality. I believe that if blacks were to finally heed a higher calling, we would turn America around today. To the 90 percent of blacks who feel that it's okay for the former president of the United States to have sex with a young girl, to lie to his administration and to the public, to encourage others to lie before a grand jury, to obstruct a federal investigation, and to allow his minions to attempt to ruin the reputations of innocent people, I say "shame on you." You are poor excuses for Americans and poor examples to your children. Blacks should take this opportunity that God has given them and make the most of it. They must learn what real forgiveness is. They must vow to become moral again.

TEACHING HATRED

Racism in the pulpit is an issue that has been ignored for the past forty years in the black churches. We hear many black preachers talking about racism in the white churches, but never the racism that is in the hearts and minds of the black preachers. We often hear black preachers say that Sunday morning is the most segregated time of the week because whites go to their churches and blacks to theirs. However, the question has never been asked, "What role are black preachers playing in keeping the races from coming together on Sunday morning?"

It is apparent to most Americans that Jesse Jackson, Maxine Waters, Louis Farrakhan, the NAACP, liberal elite whites, and the Democratic party are racists, but until now, black preachers have hidden their racism behind their pulpits. We saw an example of racism in the black churches during the last Los Angeles riots, when the Reverend Cecil Murray appeared to justify the riots as payment for white racism.

Rev. Cecil Murray, Rev. Jesse Jackson, and Minister Louis Farrakhan are not the only black ministers who carry hatred in their hearts for white people and who pass it on to their followers. The evidence is in the black community. There are churches on nearly every corner in black communities across this country, yet the black family and black life are in worse shape than they have ever been.

These pastors and others like them use their pulpits, God, and the Bible to hide the evil that lies within their hearts. They are truly the blind leading the blind. Whenever most blacks hear these pastors blame whites for their own failings, they rejoice because it takes away the responsibility of looking at themselves. The failure of blacks comes not from white people, but from hating white people. Their failure was set in motion by the failings of their own parents and their own lack of character.

Many black pastors preach one message before a white audience and then another in front of a black audience. When only blacks are around, their true hatred of whites comes out but goes uncorrected by other blacks. Blacks whose hearts are filled with hatred must be confronted and corrected, just as whites must be corrected when they are wrong.

The black churches are setting a very dangerous precedent in our country. They are leading black people down a road of total destruction.

There are blacks who interact with whites but carry a secret hatred in their hearts, which shows itself when their white associates disagree with them on racial issues. We see it all the time in the workplace. Blacks are friendly with their bosses or coworkers, but they tend to interpret any type of criticism or disagreement as racially motivated rather than as a simple difference of opinion (as they would if another black were involved). This kind of thinking is the predictable result of forty years of brainwashing by black ministers and politicians.

These "leaders" attempt to blame their hatred of whites on slavery. I grew up on a plantation in Alabama. My grandparents and parents worked the plantation, and so did I for a time. But I never saw or heard this kind of hatred from them, even though they were being discriminated against legally and socially. To blame past slavery for the actions of blacks today is a lie. Blacks are slaves only to their minds, thanks to these wicked leaders.

I am reminded of Dr. Martin Luther King Jr. when he said that people should overcome evil with good and that good would conquer all. Dr. King knew that if blacks were to wallow in hatred and blaming others for their problems, they would fail to progress. He knew they would lack the character it takes to mature, that their friends would look like enemies, and that their enemies would look like friends. We are seeing the fruits of bad seeds sown today.

Wicked pastors appear to be the friends of blacks, when in reality they are the enemy. This kind of hatred in the black churches has prevailed for so long that evil has now taken over the church. The evidence is in the acceptance of homosexuality, women having babies out of wedlock, the destruction of marriages, adultery, lying and cheating, and gang violence. Men in the churches are weaker than ever before in history. How can this be if the leader of the church is called by God and is teaching sound doctrine?

Blacks need to reject the racism that has been taught to them from the pulpit. Some blacks are angry because they feel whites do not want to marry them because of racism toward blacks. This ironically causes them to want to marry whites even more, in order to experience the thrill of getting something that they are not supposed to have. This perpetuates their struggle with racism further.

The hatred that blacks feel is causing my race to see through dark glasses. It is causing some to try to force whites to associate with them, even while they believe whites do not want to associate with them. They are clearly *becoming what they hate* and *becoming subject to what they hate.*

A good example of this is when a woman is married to a man who abuses her. She may leave him, but because of her hatred for the man, she finds herself strongly wanting him and eventually taking him back, only to encounter the same abuse. Her hatred has awakened in her an unnatural hunger for him and she becomes enslaved to him.

Nearly every black person claims to know God. Yet, when you look at the black family and community, there is no sign of God's presence. Most blacks cannot think for themselves. They think they need leaders to tell them how to think, and they believe this is normal.

It is time for our people to wake up and see that they are being used by their own ministers. The preacher has passed his or her own hatred for the white man on to them. As we know, whoever causes you to hate also controls you.

If black ministers were truly called by God, they would point the way for the people and then set them free. They would not keep the people coming and keep them in the dark through anger and deceit. In their hunger for power and wealth, they are willing to sell a person's soul down the river.

BLIND LEADING THE BLIND

I once spoke at a meeting of black preachers in Lansing, Michigan. I spoke of the control that black ministers have over black people and said that most black preachers were not called by God but by their mamas. I went on to say that these preachers should set the people free, but before I could complete my talk, I was subjected to name-calling and asked to leave the meeting in an unfriendly manner. Another time I was asked to leave a meeting in Montgomery, Alabama, because the preacher could see that my comments were making sense to his congregation. How is it that preachers claim to want to teach the truth but don't want to hear it about themselves? "[I]f the blind lead the blind, both shall fall into the ditch" (Matt. 15:14).

Dr. Martin Luther King Jr. said that one day blacks would be judged by their character and not by their color. He was right. In today's world, blacks are not judged by their color but by their *lack* of character.

In order for our community to turn around, we must take back our lives from racist ministers. Fathers need to go back to their families, learn to work hard, and guide their own children. They must drop their anger and find the truth within themselves, because the Kingdom of God is within (Luke 17:20-21), not in a building called a church. If God is capable of guiding the lives of preachers, He will likewise guide fathers and mothers, especially when they forgive and humble themselves.

AN AMAZING PHONE CALL

One day on my radio show I was taking calls, and a minister called me. I don't believe he told me his name. He was responding to a show I did pointing out some of the negative things that too many blacks are doing. I want you to see this conversation, because it is rare. Here is an unedited transcript.

> *Pastor*: My call is to apologize to you. I hung up on you a couple weeks ago.
>
> *JLP*: You're a minister, right? Yeah, I remember you.
>
> *Pastor*: I'm a pastor. As a matter of fact, I'm a bishop of three churches. I'm very sorry, and the reason I hung up on you and the reason I was angry, is I thought you were downing blacks. I listened to what you said, and I said that don't apply to me. So if it doesn't apply to me, why should I get upset about it?
>
> *JLP*: There ya go!

Pastor: So, then as I listened to what you say and look at what's around me, it's true.

JLP: Wow.

Pastor: So I just didn't have the guts to face it. But I seen it happen to my sons, and people that I know about in the neighborhood.

JLP: Yes.

Pastor: And every time they do some robbin', they're robbin' their own people.

JLP: There ya go.

Pastor: That's what I been noticing.

JLP: Yes, sir.

Pastor: But if that don't apply to me, then I shouldn't be getting upset.

JLP: Amen!

Pastor: So I can't preach and teach with something in my heart against somebody I don't even know, no how. And not only that, but I shouldn't have nothing against you or nobody else.

JLP: Well that's amazing. Your apology is accepted.

Pastor: I listened to you yesterday, and there was a lady on, and she left angry.

JLP: Yes.

Pastor: And you said, once you hung up the phone, she's gonna be listening. She might think.

JLP: That's right.

Pastor: But it took me two weeks. And I'm going to Bible study every Tuesday night and you come before my face. You know, so I just can't go around with guilt.

JLP: Wow! Well you know what, I'm in tears now. That's amazing. I'm thrown off now.

And there really isn't a lot to say after you hear that. It's amazing what God can do for us when we humble ourselves, when we let go of our pride and admit the truth. There's no freedom like the freedom truth provides. If a few more pastors would be as honest as this man, our race problems, and all our problems, would be a thing of the past.

5

Instead of Reparations, How About a Ticket Back to Africa?

—◁◁▷—

*The reparations for slavery movement is
divisive and wicked to the core*

This nation is poised for a battle that will divide us like never before. We have reaped destruction from welfare, affirmative action, Rodney King and the L.A. riots, and O.J. Simpson, but there is one battle that I'm afraid we may not recover from as a nation. That battle is for slavery "reparations."

The whole idea of reparations is racist and divisive in and of itself. It is racist in that it unfairly burdens white America with the mistakes of the past—mistakes they had nothing to do with! It is divisive because it foments rage that should have been discarded years ago. In short, the reparations movement is just another misuse of the slavery issue by the civil rights establishment to gain power and wealth.

During the last forty years, black leaders in this country seem to have grown in wealth, power, and fame, while the grievances and complaints of average black Americans have only worsened. What we need to realize is that these leaders are not working for the black community, but against it. By keeping blacks enraged at whites, their status continues to grow. But if blacks were to give up their rage, these "leaders" would no longer be necessary. That is why they drum up insidious ideas such as reparations—a plot which, I believe, will be the most destructive blacks have ever faced.

And the sad part about this is that the leaders aren't going to suffer like the average black will suffer. The black community is headed for a huge backlash brought on by a populace tired of being labeled "racists" every time they disagree with a black person.

Despite all the good that white America has done, black complaining has worsened. We asked for welfare—they gave us that. We asked for jobs—they gave us that. We asked for integrated schools—they gave us that. We asked for integrated communities—they gave us that. We asked for affirmative action—they gave us that. We asked for their women, and they even gave us that! Now we want reparations? This giving has only increased our anger, perpetuated our rage, and held us back. The only ones who seem to be succeeding among us are our "leaders" like multi-millionaire Jesse Jackson. This is how it will continue if we are given reparations.

Who will pay for reparations? I'll tell you who it will be. It will be people who don't have a racist bone in their bodies. It will be people who immigrated to this country after the Civil War. It will be people struggling to support a family. It will not be the slave owners; they're all dead. It will not be the Klansmen; most of those that are still around are so poor and backward they don't make enough money to pay the federal income taxes that will help bankroll a reparations deal.

Those who will pay for the problem will be those who never had anything to do with it. In fact, as blacks are taxpayers too, would we not be partly responsible for paying our own reparations?

Another consideration: when blacks receive reparations, will they go back to Africa? Certainly shipping blacks to America as slaves was wrong. If we undo one wrong, shouldn't we undo other wrongs as well? I know it sounds crazy, but so does the idea of reparations.

White Americans are not guilty of the sins of the past, and they must be careful not to fall to the anger of these socialist, destructive black leaders who want to racially divide and conquer us. Black Americans must drop their anger and realize that it is not the white American who is causing their destruction but their own so-called leaders, whose evil machinations know no end.

All Americans must say "no more!" to groups like the National Coalition of Blacks for Reparations in America (N'COBRA), the National Black United Front, and the Republic of New Africa that have led grassroots efforts to keep this issue alive over the past decades. America is the greatest country in the world. All men and women are free in this nation to succeed or fail, and we must no longer cave in to racism. Reparations was a wrong idea years ago, and it is a wrong idea today. It will destroy us if we don't stop it.

WHERE DO THESE CRAZY IDEAS COME FROM?

As you might expect, the absurd idea of paying blacks for the sins of slaveholders more than 150 years ago comes from the fevered minds of socialists and racist Afrocentrists who hate America and whites. Today, this whole idea of reparations is being headed by racist leaders of the black community such as Randall Robinson, former executive director of TransAfrica Forum and author of *The Debt*. It is also being pushed by U.S. Representative John Conyers (D-Michigan), who, since 1989, has unsuccessfully presented legislation calling for a study on reparations; Leonard Jeffries, a racist political science professor; and *Ebony* magazine Editor Lerone Bennett Jr.

These are just a few of the black liberal "leaders" who would rather keep blacks angry than demonstrate to them how they themselves have become successful in life. As the rest of the black community is going to hell, these men are becoming wealthy and powerful and are not thinking twice about us. If—God forbid—blacks were to receive so-called reparations, I am convinced that this money would end up in the hands of these black leaders, politicians, and lawyers, as well as many of the black ministers. In addition to solving nothing, reparations would only fuel the anger of the black community because reparations would be another failure—just as affirmative action and welfare have been.

Even before the reparations movement, there were subversives who were calling for the establishment of a separate black nation to be based in the southern states. In 1935, for example, the Communist Party USA published a pamphlet called "The Negroes in a Soviet America." The communists envisioned a "Republic of New Africa" that would include Virginia, South Carolina, Louisiana, Alabama, Arkansas, Tennessee, and other southern states.[1]

Nation of Islam leader Louis Farrakhan is a supporter of a separate black nation. In each edition of his newspaper, *The Final Call*, this racist group says, "We want our people in America whose parents or grandparents were descendants from slaves to be allowed to establish a separate state or territory of their own—either on this continent or elsewhere."

In the 1950s and 1960s, black racists Audley "Queen Mother" Moore and fugitive Robert Williams lobbied for reparations. Moore joined the Communist party in the 1930s and began a life-long war against capitalism and supporting Afrocentrism. In 1955, Moore began pushing for reparations. According to one biography, "For Moore, the issue of reparations was more than a question of assuaging any guilt white Americans harbored for the enslavement and dehumanization of African-Americans. Reparations was a constructive step in the rebuilding of African-American cultural identity—the first step in Black Nationalist ideology."[2]

Robert Williams was a criminal who fled to Cuba in 1961 after kidnapping a white couple in North Carolina. From Cuba he broadcast anti-American speeches through "Radio Free Dixie." In his broadcast and newsletter, he urged blacks to kill police and other public officials. He also called for slavery reparations as part of a "national liberation movement" against so-called American colonial powers.[3]

This Marxist-inspired call for black reparations has been picked up by N'COBRA, Jackson, Robinson, and Rep. Conyers.

N'COBRA has published its demands on its web site, www.NCO-BRA.com:

> We want our just inheritance: the trillions of dollars due us for the labors of our ancestors who worked for hundreds of years without pay. We demand the resources required removing all badges and indicia of slavery.

To be specific:

> Payment may include all of the following: land, equipment, factories, licenses, banks, ships, airplanes, various forms of tax relief, education & training, to name a few.

N'COBRA also claims that this is not just an issue for America, but says that blacks around the world are owed reparations from their European colonizers!

The reparations movement had largely been limited to black racist fringe groups until 2000. But then the movement started to go mainstream. Contributing to this mainstreaming effort was the publication of Randall Robinson's book, *The Debt: What America Owes to Blacks*. Robinson has managed to parlay this insane idea into a full-time career. He appears on TV and radio talk shows and travels throughout the United States giving speeches at colleges on reparations.

Robinson's book reveals his pro-Marxist tendencies, his hatred of America, and his love for Fidel Castro's communist dictatorship. In fact, he devotes an entire chapter to praising Castro and the tyranny he has created for the Cuban people. In his chapter on Castro and Cuba, Robinson recalls his 1999 visit to that island. He describes America's embargo of Cuba as a "crucifixion" and describes Castro as "an inferno of intellect and determination" who is "connecting Cuba's racial past to its present."[4]

I had a very heated discussion about reparations not long ago on my radio show with Dorothy Tillman, a black activist and Chicago Alderwoman. Tillman was at one time an organizer for Dr. Martin Luther King Jr.'s organization in Alabama but moved to Chicago years ago to become a radical force for liberalism there.

Tillman pushed through an ordinance in October 2002 that required companies doing business with the city to document if they ever profited from slavery. Undoubtedly, her goal is to gather information on these companies so that the reparations crowd can sue them for millions.

Tillman told me,

> We've been working hard and long on the reparations movement and you know we're stuck in some posttraumatic slavery syndrome and that a lot of residue of slavery still exists. We know that we have had the Indians, the Jewish community, the Japanese community, people all over the world have received reparations but the descendants of slaves— Africans in America—haven't. . . . America cannot deny that they owe us and we built this country. Black labor [built] this nation and wealth was handed down to white descendants and poverty down to us.

I tried to get her to explain more about this "posttraumatic slavery syndrome" as the cause of black crime, high abortion rates, and illegitimacy rates among blacks. She managed to blame all of these things on whites or on this nonexistent syndrome that she insists is real. In Tillman's mind, it seemed like every negative behavior that blacks exhibit is apparently what she calls a "residue" of slavery—so blacks personally are never at fault for their own behavior. At one point she accused me of suffering from this posttraumatic slavery syndrome and said she felt like she was talking to a patient who needed treatment!

She even claimed that black-on-black crime is the result of the residue of posttraumatic slave syndrome. I was amazed at the nonsense she was spewing—but she's considered a leader in the reparations movement and is a power to be reckoned with in Chicago. God help that city!

The reparations movement is making some frightening gains, and its strategy for accumulating power is simple: in Washington, D.C., Cleveland, Dallas, Detroit, Chicago, and other cities, black racists have managed to get resolutions passed that recommend "restitution" for slavery. It begins with conducting "studies" of insurance companies and banks to see if these corporations ever profited from slavery. What begins with seemingly harmless studies will eventually be converted into lawsuits against these corporations for their alleged role in slavery.

The reparations movement was handed a significant victory in California in 2001, thanks to the work of radical socialist state senator Tom Hayden (D-CA). Hayden, of course, is a former leader in the violent Students for a Democratic Society (SDS) and was married to pro-Viet Cong actress Jane Fonda.

Hayden sponsored two pieces of legislation that advanced the reparations movement. California's extremist liberal Governor Gray Davis signed both into law in October 2000. Both laws, "Slaverholder Insurance Policies Bill" and "Slavery Colloquium Bill," are designed to research the history of insurance companies and their involvement with slavery.

Shortly after Davis signed these laws, black racists announced the formation of a Reparations Assessment Group (RAG). This group is composed of a dream team of radical lawyers who are developing strategies for suing America's businesses for billions of dollars for their alleged involvement in slavery, including O.J. Simpson attorney Johnnie Cochran, TransAfrica's Randall Robinson, Harvard Law Professor Charles J. Ogletree, and others. These men see dollar signs and will exploit this fraudulent issue as long as they can.

RAG filed its first class action lawsuit against three major companies in March of 2002. RAG has targeted AETNA; CSX, a railroad company; and FleetBoston, a banking firm. According to Ogletree, "We want a change in America. We want full recognition and a remedy of how slavery stigmatized, raped, murdered and exploited millions of Africans through no fault of their own."[5]

RAG plans to file similar lawsuits, supposedly on behalf of 35 million descendants of slaves against more than 100 corporations in the future. The ultimate goal is to shake money from the trees of these businesses and then target the federal government for an even larger monetary shakedown.

A LITTLE LESSON ABOUT SLAVERY

The socialists and racists who are pushing for reparations couldn't care less about the real history of slavery throughout human history, but those interested in the truth need a mini-lesson about this horrible crime against humanity.

In Africa, for example, warring black tribes typically enslaved their captives, killed some, and sold others into slavery for profit. The Muslims also ran a lucrative slave trade long before the white man ever reached Africa.

Historian Kevin Beary detailed the horrendous black slave-trading business that existed in the 17th and 18th centuries in Africa. He noted the observations of a slave trader named Captain William Snelgrave, who published a book in 1734 about his experiences buying and selling slaves. In his book, Snelgrave described the practice of black tribesmen making slaves of their war captives and observed that many of these slaves were simply killed because they frequently had more than they could use on their own plantations.[6]

In former slave trader John Newton's book, *Thoughts upon the African Slave Trade*, he writes that,

> The [African] law . . . punishes some species of theft with slavery; and in cases of adultery, both the woman, and the man who offends with her are liable to be sold for slaves. . . . I believe many of the slaves purchased in Sherbo, and probably upon the whole Windward coast, are convicts, who have forfeited their liberty, by breaking the laws of their country. I judge, the principal source of the slave trade, is the wars which prevail among the natives.[7]

Another slave trader named Captain Theophilus Conneau published a book in 1754 that described his life as a slaver. In his chapter, "How the Free Black Becomes a Slave," Conneau wrote:

> In Africa, where coin is not known, the slave is made a substitute for this commodity. Therefore, if a man wants to purchase a wife, he pays the amount in slaves; another wishes to purchase a quantity in cattle, he tenders in payment slaves. Fields of cassava, rice, or yams are paid in slaves. The African court also taxes all forfeitures and pecuniary penalties in slaves.[8]

Says Beary, "We Americans are not responsible for the African slave tradition. We did not begin slavery, we ended it. As many disturbing reports from modern Africa show, slavery has still not been wholly eradicated from that continent."[9]

Indeed, instead of focusing on slavery that was abolished in America more than 150 years ago, why don't these leaders spend time fighting to abolish slavery that still exists in Africa?

Ironically, the opposite is true. Several years ago, a coalition of Christian conservatives and Jewish groups got together to begin drawing national attention to the current-day horrors of slavery in African and Muslim nations. Charles Jacobs, a Jewish man who heads the American Anti-Slavery Group, says his organization first went to liberals for help in fighting against African slavery.

According to Jacobs, "We started out going to the left. We thought: Let's go to all the people who fought apartheid. Let's go to the women's groups. Let's go to black leaders. Let's go to liberal journalists, liberal churches, progressive peoples, human rights organizations. But the left rejected us. Jesse Jackson's office told me he wouldn't touch it because it could be perceived as an anti-Arab campaign."[10]

Jacobs and others in the anti-slavery movement say liberals like Jackson are uncomfortable with the fact that current-day slave masters in Sudan are black Muslims, not white Christians. To denounce the slavery practiced by black Muslims in Sudan would outrage extremists like Louis Farrakhan. Apparently some forms of slavery are acceptable as long as the slave masters are the right color and religion.

The incredible silence of black leaders over the present day atrocities being committed in Africa by black Muslims says a lot about the hypocrisy of these racists—and tells a great deal about their real agendas in demanding reparations for something that happened more than 150 years ago. They're after money, power, and the perpetuation of racial strife.

When *Washington Times* reporter Bill Sammon called Louis Farrakhan's office to get a statement about African slavery, his call was not returned. Farrakhan's followers claim that African slavery is a fiction created by Jewish conspirators who wish to destroy Islam. But Samuel Cotton, a black man who heads up the Coalition Against Slavery in Mauritania and Sudan, told Sammon: "White Republicans are really the only individuals who have fought and put together any legislation for the abolition of slavery. The black intelligentsia, politicians, and spiritual leaders manifest no interest toward this."[11]

Reparations advocate Randall Robinson, for example, has no interest in fighting against black Muslim slavery in Africa or elsewhere. The truth of the matter is that Randall Robinson's friend Fidel Castro has held more than 11 million people (the population of Cuba) in virtual slavery since 1959 and has murdered thousands of men, women, and children who have resisted him. Yet Robinson wants those of us who had nothing to do with slavery in the 19th century to pay out an estimated $8 trillion in reparations for supposedly benefiting from slavery.

Thomas Sowell, a distinguished black economist and political columnist, has written extensively on the idiocy of reparations and the damage it will do to race relations and to our economy. According to Sowell:

> The first thing to understand about the issue of reparations for slavery is that no money is going to be paid. The very people who are demanding reparations know it is not going to happen.
>
> Why then are they demanding something that they know they are

not going to get? Because the demagogues themselves will benefit, even if nobody else does. Stirring up historic grievances pays off in publicity and votes.[12]

THE REACTION

In April 2002, I decided it was time to take to the road to fight against the growing threat of the reparations movement. I launched my "Stop Reparations NOW!" speaking tour in June.

I was invited in August to attend the annual conference of the National Association of Black Journalists (NABJ) to debate the issue of reparations with University of Pennsylvania's Afrocentrist professor, Michael Dyson.

Dyson is a darling of the liberal left in America. He has written a positive book about the late rap artist Tupac Shakur, whom he calls a "ghetto saint." Shakur, for the record, was a street thug, a hater of women, and a promoter of violence. Only in the mind of a corrupt liberal like Dyson could he be considered any sort of saint. After the September 11, 2001, terrorist attack on our nation, Dyson went so far as to say that it was "predictable to a degree due to America's past imperialistic practices."[13]

The reparations debate, hosted by NABJ president Condace Pressley, was poorly organized from the beginning, and it was clear to me that I was in hostile territory.

Someone from NABJ was supposed to pick me up from the airport, but no one came until my office called and complained. No one was assigned to show me around or to introduce me to other guests at the conference, and at the end of the meeting, I was even told I'd have to pay for my meal—after they'd already indicated that they'd cover it. Again, my office had to fight for that.

I've spoken in front of organizations across America in the nation's biggest cities. I've been treated very well in most cases. But I must say I have never been treated so poorly or unprofessionally as I was by the National Association of Black Journalists at this conference.

Dyson arrived thirty minutes late to the debate, yet he was allowed to make both the opening and closing statements. During Dyson's statement, he blamed whites for the high incarceration rates of black males and said that white America was responsible for a host of other serious social problems. He received thunderous applause from the journalists.

In my opening statement, I told these journalists that black Americans didn't need reparations. What they needed were intact, two-parent homes with good fathers leading them. I told them that blacks are not suffering from racism but from lack of moral character. I also said that while education is important for blacks, education alone will not repair the moral and physical damage that has been done to blacks over the past forty years by fraudulent civil rights leaders. My words were met with boos, jeers, and laughter.

During the Q&A session, NABJ Co-Founder Vernon Jarrett took the microphone and scornfully asked me, "Are you for real? Do you believe what you're saying? You're just a pawn of the white man. You have this little white boy [indicating my assistant] running around passing out your newsletters." I answered Jarrett's insults by saying, "I'm saddened by your statements. Normally, when people get older, they gain wisdom. But you're an old fool." I then had my assistant, Doug Massey, who is a light-skinned black man, stand up so the audience could see him. Jarrett then came back at me with a childish response: "Don't get me started—I'll talk about your mama!" This is from a man who is billed as one of the nation's foremost media commentators about race. I was amazed.

During the Q&A, black journalists attacked my educational background and speech, and I was accused of being a pawn and "white man's boy." This treatment came from a group of blacks who are supposedly trained to be fair-minded journalists.

Dyson was so angered by my statements that he wrote a scathing article about me in the *Chicago Sun-Times*, accusing me of "worshipping at the altar of whiteness" and of being a "self-hating" black man, among many more accusations.[14]

Dyson's attacks turned out to be one of the best things he could have done for me. After the *Sun-Times* article appeared, I was inundated with media requests for interviews to tell my side of the story. The *Washington Times* picked up the story, and after that I was invited on numerous TV and talk shows, including "Voice of America," where I fielded calls from as far away as Africa. Sean Hannity, a BOND Advisory Board member, had me on his Fox News Channel show, "Hannity and Colmes." Hannity also invited Dyson to appear.

During this encounter, Dyson accused me of spewing out "the most venomous, vindictive, hateful venom" and said I was "reprehensible" for saying blacks are immoral and lack character.[15] Something had stuck in his craw. What really fried Dyson was that late in the interview I told him, an ordained Baptist minister with a Ph.D. in religion from Princeton, that he didn't know God. I meant it, and it hit him hard. Dyson definitely hated me, and much like the pastor that I mentioned last chapter who called my radio show to apologize, his hatred was causing me to stay at the forefront of his mind.

As proof of that, many months later when the issue should have long blown over in his mind, Dyson wrote another scathing column about me in *Savoy*, a black culture magazine. His *Savoy* article was titled, "I'm Gonna Get You, Sucka."

According to Dyson: "Peterson is a racial parasite. That's a species of race-man in reverse, a black person obsessed with pointing out black people's racial obsessions. By claiming that black people rely too much on race to explain their troubles, the racial parasite gains attention and, thus, relies on those blacks to make a living." He closed the article by simply saying, "Nigga, please!"[16]

Liberal elitists like Dyson are threatened by me because they know I'm revealing the lie so people can see the truth. Dyson would like to believe he can hide from the truth behind his wall of intellectualism. Deep down he knows he can't, and that really bothers him. That's why he doesn't address my claims but attacks me personally.

Another time I was invited to speak to a rabidly pro-reparations group in Los Angeles. The lady who had set up the talk, well-known in the black community as "Pearl Jr.," had already harangued me at a

Q&A session when I spoke at another Saturday morning gathering at an Inglewood, California, coffee shop, which was moderated by Earl Ofari Hutchinson. (Earl and I have never seen eye to eye on most issues—he's pretty far to the left—but he has always treated me respectfully and fairly, and I appreciate that decency.) The place I was to talk was, interestingly, Rev. Robinson-Gaither's church, the man I spoke of in the previous chapter who encouraged homosexuality and who had Geronimo Pratt speak at his church, as well as hosting legal planning for the LA-4, the thugs accused of beating and causing numerous fractures to the skull of motorist Reginald Denny during the L.A. riots.

My "Stop Reparations NOW!" speech went over like a lead balloon in front of these folks. We had been videotaping the speech, partly for posterity and partly for security, when an elderly woman in the front demanded we stop taping. After some discussion, we agreed we'd turn off the camera. No sooner had we done so than the woman stood up and yelled at me, "If you were my son, I'd shoot you!"

That's certainly not the first time I've heard that kind of talk. I've been threatened several times with a gun. Once after the L.A. riots, I was invited to a town hall meeting for "Nightline with Ted Koppel." When Koppel approached me and asked, "What is the problem in the black community?" I stood up in an auditorium packed with angry black folks, pointed at Congresswoman Maxine Waters, and said, "Maxine Waters is the problem in the black community!" Not surprisingly, Koppel turned another shade whiter than his usual, abruptly turned away, and never came back to me. I was followed out of the studio that night by two young black men. One pulled a gun and told me I'd better watch my back. I asked him why. He told me it was because of what I'd said about Maxine and other black leaders.

Despite threats, the truth remains: paying reparations for slavery is ridiculous. But as I have said before, only liberal intellectuals are crazy enough to accept this idea as reasonable and as something that actually should be done. Reparations will intensify racial antagonism and generate new levels of racial resentment. It will alienate blacks from the mainstream and create more racial hatred than has ever existed before.

REPARATIONS HAVE ALREADY BEEN PAID

The fact is that only a small minority of Americans ever owned slaves. In the pre-Civil War South, only one white in five was a slave owner. So why should the descendants of non-slaveholding whites owe a debt? There are also descendents of the 350,000 union soldiers who died to free the slaves. Haven't they already paid, with their own blood?

Another fact that is ignored is that most Americans living today are the descendants of post-Civil War immigrants, who have no lineal connection to slavery at all. So why should these people—who had no involvement in slavery—be forced to pay for something that occurred 150 years ago? And why should today's blacks—who have not suffered from any consequences of slavery—be given checks for something that may have happened to their great-great-grandparents more than a century ago?

Blacks should ask themselves what debt they owe to whites—both Americans and British—who lobbied and fought and died to bring an end to slavery, a practice that has gone on for as long as the human race has existed.

Where is there any historical evidence that Muslims or African tribal chiefs have ever been overly concerned about their practice of enslaving and/or killing their enemies? It was whites—not Muslims, blacks, American Indians, Chinese, or members of any other ethnicity or race—that fought to end slavery in the 19th century. The fact is that Arabs, African tribal chiefs, and other ethnic groups still routinely enslave men, women, and children and traffic in slaves. Whites like William Wilberforce in England and William Lloyd Garrison in America were the ones who spearheaded the anti-slavery movement and created the political and moral pressure in Britain and America to bring an end to this horrible practice.

For blacks who live in the most opportunity-rich country in human history to demand money for the sins of 150 years ago is absolutely shameful. For white Americans, or any Americans—many of whose ancestors weren't even in this country at the time of slavery—to pay reparations is a deep injustice.

The effect of reparations would be among the most devastating blows the country and the black community have ever experienced. There would be hell to pay—we would see an unparalleled backlash. Whites and blacks would be divided like never before. But you don't hear Jesse Jackson ever talk about this inevitable catastrophe—and he's supposed to be a leader with the well-being of black Americans first in his mind.

I must say that I don't believe reparations will end up being paid out. Most whites don't want to pay money to atone for something they're not guilty of, and most blacks have sense enough to see through this nonsense. But the very fact that we are seriously allowing this ridiculous debate is itself divisive and inflammatory.

It is time that all Americans of goodwill stand up and say "No more!" Unless we want to see division like never before, and the utter destruction of the black community, we must stop reparations now.

6

White Fear

—ɱ—

How white cowardice hurts blacks

For the last thirteen years, we at the Brotherhood Organization of A New Destiny have been fighting against the demoralization of blacks in this country from the likes of Jesse Jackson, Maxine Waters, Louis Farrakhan, Al Sharpton, the Black Caucus, the liberal elite of the Democratic party, and others. But we must realize that this is not the only form of demoralization at work. While demoralizing blacks, these racist demagogues have also succeeded in demoralizing whites.

The threat of being labeled "racist" causes whites to cower to the wishes of blacks and hold their tongues when they see things amiss in the black community. The fact is that the civil rights "leaders" and elite liberal Democrats are much at fault for the poor condition of the black community, not so-called white racists. But, having largely given in to their lies, white culture is suffering, not only because blacks are free to be immoral without complaint but also because many whites now lack character as a result of giving in to this fear for so long.

As whites allowed themselves to be paralyzed from fear, legitimate black leaders were pushed aside by racial scam artists. These phony leaders then consolidated power over blacks, and the result has been an ever-increasing level of immorality within the black community.

Compounding the problem, the sins of the parents are passed down through the generations. As a result of whites not standing up in the past, this same weakness and lack of character is repeated in the new generation. The idea of being called "racist" is as horrific to them as ever, and whites of the new generation have been silenced because of their parents' poor example.

CREATING FEAR

In order to change, we must first realize how we came to the problem we find ourselves in today. Black leaders and their Democratic party cohorts understand one thing very well: the power of fear. For the last forty years, these demagogues have implanted one all-encompassing fear in the white community—fear of being branded "racist." As this fear escalated in the beginning of this movement, whites became afraid and refused to speak against the civil rights movement as it veered from its original just intent. While still accomplishing some good, it became a self-serving and racist agenda shortly after the death of Dr. Martin Luther King Jr.

I'm often asked to speak on college campuses where white kids are afraid to stand up to immoral blacks for fear of being labeled bigots, and they are afraid to express their Christianity for fear of being labeled homophobic.

As a result of this fear, college graduates go into the world demoralized and disillusioned, depressed, and beaten down. Their hearts are filled with fear and helplessness, perpetrated on them by the "celebrate diversity" crowd. And unless this changes, this will pass on to the next generation, and the next, and we will all suffer. These days most whites believe that being labeled a racist is the worst form of suffering. The dark days lurking ahead will make that suffering look like nothing. But it does not—I repeat, does not—have to be this way!

We at BOND realize the suffering that our nation is going through is a type of warfare. What we all have to realize, though, is that this is not *racial* warfare but *spiritual* warfare. It is not a fight of blacks versus whites, as the civil rights movement will tell you, but of good versus evil. Leaders of the evil civil rights movement attack good Americans who speak out against what they are doing. But the civil rights movement has no real power. All it can do is create fear through name-calling. And, amazingly, most whites have given in to this. They have adopted a false guilt for the ills of the black community.

The civil rights "leaders" and Democratic party are truly to blame, holding blacks down and dependent on the government by keeping them angry at white America. God, family, country, morality, and discipline used to be paramount in black culture, which is why blacks such as Booker T. Washington flourished long ago, even though laws discriminated against blacks. Now diversity, multiculturalism, and governmental programs are paramount, and look where blacks are because of it. We now have a society where blacks can say anything they want about whites, but whites can't even speak up and disagree with blacks.

Taking a stand for what is right has put me at odds with the civil rights establishment. I have endured all kinds of name-calling and intimidation tactics. I have personally been called "nigger," "sellout," "Uncle Tom," and many other names. But I understand that I am fighting against evil. These names mean nothing to me. They are the pitiful words of cowards who do not have right on their side. By letting them pass, I am able to continue standing up for what is right: the emancipation of black America and the disbandment of the current black leadership.

It is now time for white Americans to realize that they are part of this same battle. Enduring these attacks is part of a blessed life. I know that whenever a person stands up for right he will be subject to such attacks.

If Americans of all races can lay aside their fear and stand up for truth, we will all be blessed. If they do not lay aside this fear, then destruction will be widespread.

THE LESSON OF LOTT

The national humiliation and rejection that befell former Senate Majority Leader Trent Lott (R-MS) in December of 2002 is a tragic reminder of the immense power of black racists and white fear.

Senator Lott was making some offhand comments at a party celebrating the 100th birthday of the late Senator Strom Thurmond (R-SC). In an attempt to compliment Thurmond, Lott made the following remarks:

> I want to say this about my state: When Strom Thurmond ran for president, we voted for him. We're proud of it. And if the rest of the country had followed our lead, we wouldn't have had all these problems over all these years, either.

That's when all hell broke loose. Black racists immediately grabbed this comment as Lott's secretly coded message to KKK and Aryan Nation types that he wished our nation were still segregated.

Strom Thurmond had run for the presidency in 1948 as a Dixiecrat on a segregationist platform. Lott's comment was seized as an opportunity for black racists and their white liberal power brokers in the media and in Congress to draw blood from the newly-elected Republican majority in the Senate.

Not only did liberals and black racists launch a relentless assault against Lott, but even Ken Connor of the Family Research Council issued a press release blasting Lott for his thoughtless remarks. Connor noted: "Words matter, despite what may have been in Senator Lott's mind when he spoke. And the senator's words, in the ears of black Americans, sound unmistakably like a repudiation of desegregation and the civil rights movement."[1]

Lott repeatedly apologized for his remarks and even went on Black Entertainment Television (BET) to repent of his ill-considered comments, but the damage was done. He lost the support of President Bush, and his fellow Republican senators began to realize that he was irreparably damaged by his statement. Ironically, he never would have been invited on BET to discuss any issues before this occurred. BET was just trying to exploit his poor choice of words to attack the Republican party and to tar it as a party of racism. It is regrettable that President Bush failed to stand up for him.

I issued a press release in support of Senator Lott on December 12, 2002, and went on as many talk shows as I could to show solidarity and forgiveness for Lott's remarks. In my press release I observed:

> As the head of a nationally recognized nonprofit black organization, BOND, the Brotherhood Organization of a New Destiny, my organization and I accept Senator Trent Lott's apology regarding his remarks at Senator Strom Thurmond's birthday celebration. I encourage the Senator to not give into the demands of racists who want to keep blacks on the Democratic plantation.
>
> . . . Black and white Democrats alike who continue to demand that he [Lott] step down are doing so only for political reasons. And Republicans who fail to support him are displaying cowardice. Lott should not step down; he should not offer any more apologies—this matter is done! We should judge people based on their hearts and actions, and unlike many of his detractors, Trent Lott has no history of being a racist.

I predicted early on in this controversy that even if Trent Lott killed himself to make amends for his misstatement, this wouldn't be enough for the black racists and liberal crowd. They would rejoice at his death and continue to blame the Republican party for its alleged history of racism or insensitivity to liberal black causes. Fortunately, Lott has chosen to remain alive and continues to serve in the Senate, even though he did resign as Senate Majority Leader.

I was correct about the black racists who would not let go of this issue. Bob Herbert, a hate-filled black liberal columnist for the *New*

York Times, launched a major attack against the Republican party in a column published only a day after Lott resigned.

In his racist rant, Herbert claims that Lott's problem isn't going to go away for the Republican party "because Republican leaders haven't rid themselves of the habit of playing to the closet racists and the Confederate flag-waving yahoos who mean so much to the GOP. For forty years the party has gone out of its way to court the enemies of black people. It's an offense for which it should be begging forgiveness."[2]

Herbert goes on to claim that the GOP has no intention of cleansing itself from the "taint" of racism. He also makes the absurd charge that the GOP has spent thirty years "stomping on the voting rights of blacks" and trying to pack the courts with individuals who are hostile to the supposed interests of minorities. Herbert seems to have trouble distinguishing between truth and falsehood, and he has a long history of demonizing the Republican party as the worst evil ever to befall our nation. He's been playing this racist tune for years in his columns.

I invited Los Angeles Congresswoman Diane Watson on my radio show during the Lott controversy to get her opinion on his statement and apology. She gave the typical leftist spin. She condemned Trent Lott, but when I asked her why there was no outcry from Democrats over Senator Robert Byrd's comments about "white niggers" or his past membership in the KKK, she said, "You're hearing an outcry from me, Diane Watson, a Democrat out of California, about a statement that Trent Lott made. And I'm not going to speak for Democrats about that statement [Byrd's reference to white niggers]." Obviously, it's okay to be a former KKK member and use the word "nigger" as a U.S. Senator—as long as you're a loyal liberal Democrat! But woe to a Republican who might slip up. The fires of hell will be unleashed upon you as they were on Trent Lott.

WHITE FEAR—AND SWIFT PUNISHMENT

What happened to Trent Lott because of an ill-conceived statement sends a strong message to any white person who dares utter a word to oppose black racist crackpots. The professional victims have so successfully used the "racism" label on their opponents that it is extremely difficult for any white to stand up to them.

These leaders have positioned themselves in such a way that if a white person opposes any liberal program supposedly aimed at helping blacks, that white person is automatically considered a racist. If you oppose affirmative action, you're a racist (if you're black and oppose affirmative action, you're a "house nigger" or an "Uncle Tom"). If you oppose welfare programs that result in dependency and laziness, you're a racist. If you oppose Afrocentric history classes that tell lies about blacks, you're a racist. If you oppose "racial norming" in school test scores, you're a racist. If you're against condom distribution programs in inner cities, you're not only a racist, but you're in favor of genocide against blacks because you're supposedly helping to spread the AIDS virus.

The list goes on and on, but you get the point. Conservatives like myself are put in a position of being labeled racists whenever we oppose these sorts of proposals. In short, the black racists have assumed a position of superiority and have appointed themselves judges of our culture. If they propose a plan for "helping" blacks, no matter its actual outcome, then their plan must be carried out and all criticism must be quashed. Black racists define what is good and true, what is moral and immoral. Their acts and thoughts are good and moral; those who oppose them are by nature evil and must be destroyed if possible. If you oppose a liberal racist program, you risk being tarred and feathered and run out of town on a rail.

I speak to a lot of white people as I travel around this country, and I often ask them to raise their hands if they're afraid of speaking the truth about blacks. I get a lot of raised hands, and I'm sure that I would get more, but many of them are too afraid even to admit this. I find this to be a consistent fear in both Christian and non-Christian audiences.

Whites have been so terrorized by the politically correct crowd that even when no racism is intended, a white person can find himself crucified by the professional racists. One of the most ridiculous examples is when a white aide to the newly elected black mayor of Washington, D.C., was in a staff meeting and used the word "niggardly" to describe something. Word immediately got out that the man was a closet racist, and some were demanding his resignation. Instead of simply telling his critics to *get a dictionary* to learn the real definition of the word he had used, the man apologized for his comment and resigned. Withering under the ignorant assault on his aide, the black mayor refused to defend him. (He later re-hired him after conservative pundits heavily criticized the mayor.)[3]

When liberal racists utter despicable statements against whites or black conservatives, there is no outcry against them. No liberals rose up in anger at Michael Dyson, for example, for calling me a "self-loathing" black because I oppose reparations. There is an understood agreement among liberals that no tactic is too immoral, no statement is too harsh, and no ridicule is too intense for anyone who opposes the liberal racial agenda.

My good friend Ezola Foster, a courageous black conservative who heads Americans for Family Values, has recounted her experiences dealing with conservative-haters.

I spent 17 years as an activist in the Democrat Party before I came to the conclusion that the left wing that controls the Party is motivated not by a love of the oppressed, but rather by hatred for the values I cherish and those who defend them.

"We must hate," Bolshevik leader Vladimir Lenin exhorted his followers. "Hatred is the essence of communism." Lenin gathered around him a movement of those who regarded themselves as victims and who were motivated by hatred for Russian society; once the Bolsheviks came to power they created a regime that left behind tens of millions of corpses and the ruins of a wrecked nation. America's Establishment-anointed "Black Leaders"—Jesse Jackson, Louis Farrakhan, Maxine Waters, and others—faithfully follow Lenin's destructive blueprint.[4]

Mrs. Foster is right on target with her analysis of the black racists who have positioned themselves as the new rulers over American blacks. No deviation from liberal orthodoxy is permitted or you'll be relentlessly hounded, ridiculed, and hated.

WHITE GUILT—AND BAD POLICIES

Black English Professor Shelby Steele describes what he calls "white guilt" and the impact that this guilt has had in hampering black progress in America. Writing in *The Content of Our Character*, Steele says that he believes that the guilt experienced by many white Americans in the 1960s led to the passage of many laws and policies that were designed to expiate this guilt. But these policies led to programs that actually have harmed black progress during the past forty years.

Steele notes that various entitlement programs—affirmative action, for example—have done little to help blacks gain skills and independence. "One of the effects of entitlements, I believe," says Steele, "has been to encourage in blacks a dependency both on the entitlements and on the white guilt that generates them." There may be perceived benefits here, but as Steele warns, "Even when it serves ideal justice, bounty from another man's guilt weakens."[5]

In an essay published in the the *Wall Street Journal*, Steele lamented the fact that "white guilt" has paralyzed whites from openly speaking the truth about black social ailments:

> White guilt is best understood as a vacuum of moral authority. Whites live with this vacuum despite the fact that they may not feel a trace of personal guilt over past oppression of blacks. Whites simply come to a place with blacks where they feel no authority to speak or judge and where they sense a great risk of being seen as racist. It is a simple thing, this lack of authority, but it has changed everything. One terrible feature is that it means whites lack the authority to say what they see when looking at blacks and black problems.[6]

President Bush has provided leadership toward lessening white fear. The Bush administration has imposed economic sanctions on Zimbabwean President Robert Mugabe and seventy-six other high-ranking government officials, whom the U.S. accuses of undermining democracy. Bush issued an executive order freezing their assets and barred Americans from engaging in any transactions or dealings with them.

Mugabe is a vicious tyrant who is infamous for having mandated a policy of forcibly seizing the farmland of white citizens in Zimbabwe (formerly white-majority Rhodesia) and giving it to blacks, particularly friends of his regime. His policy has encouraged violence—resulting even in murder—against those white citizens. His country has fallen into economic crisis and famine in large part due to this seizure.

But don't look for much criticism from other quarters. The "civil rights" leadership in America has barely raised a sound against the brutal Mugabe's crimes against white farmers or reported widespread violence against the black-led Movement for Democratic Change, led by Morgan Tsvangirai, which strongly opposes the dictator. Instead, it is President Bush whom these racist leaders oppose. Not surprisingly, Bush's strong leadership was immediately condemned by an unnamed Zimbabwean official as part of a "white racist" attack on Zimbabwe!

Whites must reject white fear if there is to be any real progress in overthrowing the totalitarian hold that socialist black scam artists have over blacks in this country. It is time to break free of the stranglehold that fear has imposed over whites. It is time for truth-telling and for the national repudiation of corrupt leaders like Jackson, Farrakhan, Sharpton, Waters, etc. If white Americans do not face and overcome white fear, they can expect someday to face the same treatment the white farmers in Zimbabwe are receiving today.

7

Repudiating Jesse Jackson

—◊◊◊—

Jesse Jackson is a racist demagogue,
a problem profiteer of the highest order

I had the displeasure of encountering Jesse Jackson and his cohorts during a December 10, 2001, meeting at the Los Angeles Chamber of Commerce, sponsored by Jackson's Rainbow/PUSH Trade Bureau. Toyota's vice president of corporate communications, Irv Miller, was meeting with Jackson's team and approximately two to three hundred mostly black businessmen and women to explain his company's "21st Century Diversity Strategy" and its budget of $700 million, targeted to minority communities.

The background motivation is more interesting: the corporate version of white fear.

Miller showed up and gave his spiel to appease because Jackson raised a stink about a Toyota advertisement that he claimed was deeply offensive to blacks. The ad featured a black man with a gold RAV4

Toyota sport utility vehicle embossed on his front tooth. In response to the ad, Jackson said, "The only thing missing is the watermelon." Jackson, of course, sees racism whenever there is an opportunity for a shakedown of a major corporation. Seeing his chance, he was on Toyota like ugly on an ape. The company kowtowed.

I almost did not attend the meeting, but my director of public relations, Ermias Alemayehu, urged me to go. I arrived in my stylish-but-casual BOND fleece jacket; almost all the businessmen in attendance wore suits. We took seats at the very front of the room.

Once the meeting started, it was evident that it was "The Jesse Jackson Show." Jackson had the microphone for the majority of the time, and he ran the meeting. He asked for a show of hands of all in attendance who were members of his trade bureau, and then asked for the hands of those who were not members of the bureau. After that, Jackson had each member of his trade bureau from the panel and audience (except those at the head table) stand up and state his or her name, company name, and type of business. Naturally, Rainbow/PUSH trade bureau membership applications were available just outside the main doors. Joining Jackson's bureau costs businesses from $250-$2,500 per year, depending on how much money a company grosses.

Jackson and others at the meeting said that by joining Jackson's trade bureau, a business would have many doors opened to it, including opportunities to do business with companies including Toyota and BMW. BMW was mentioned by name as a company that Rainbow/PUSH would be going after next. The implication was strong that joining the trade bureau would make a company eligible to receive contracts with Toyota. Therefore, Jackson had, in effect, set himself up as the gatekeeper of the contracts. Irv Miller of Toyota never contradicted this impression during the meeting.

When it came time to make the hard close and collect the money, Jackson had an associate give a fiery sermon-like speech, letting the assembled know how much Jackson has done for blacks and how he has sacrificed to serve. It was a very hard sell, and the Jackson team went from table to table collecting checks. They also collected money for Jackson's upcoming sixtieth birthday bash at the Beverly Hilton Hotel.

This took place with no protest or comment from Toyota.

As further demonstration of his power, Jackson introduced a man seated at the head table named J.L. Armstrong, a Rainbow/PUSH member who works for Toyota, and announced that Armstrong was being promoted to head Toyota's supplier development, meaning he would be the point man between black business beneficiaries and Toyota. Jackson took responsibility for Armstrong's promotion, again without dispute from Miller of Toyota.

An announcement months later of Armstrong's promotion verified the purpose of his new position: "He is responsible for managing the company's progress of purchases from minority- and women-owned firms."[1]

Irv Miller conducted a multimedia presentation explaining Toyota's "21st Century Diversity Program." I could see in watching Mr. Miller how afraid he appeared, and I felt sorry for him. I thought to myself, and later remarked in media appearances, that this must be the weakest white man I'd ever seen!

After it was completed, there was a question and answer session. I stood up and introduced myself and my organization BOND. I said that, curiously, whenever Jesse Jackson is involved in a shakedown of a corporation, he never helps conservative black organizations like BOND. Already, I was hearing loud, rude remarks and derisive laughter from the pro-Jackson crowd.

I told Miller that we had a Home for Boys program and asked how an organization like ours could work with Toyota without having to go through Jesse Jackson and Rainbow/PUSH.

At this point, all hell broke loose in the room. Several blacks got up and started screaming obscenities at me. Judge Greg Mathis, who has his own TV show, "The Judge Mathis Show," yelled at me and said, "Oh, you've been watching too much TV. You've been watching too much [Fox News Channel's Bill] O'Reilly."

"Well, at least I don't watch your boring show," I said.

Jackson crony Carl Dickerson, one of the meeting's hosts, called me stupid and told me to sit down.

Once order was somewhat restored, Jonathan Jackson (one of Jesse's sons) and another man came down and tried to intimidate me.

They sat down directly across from me in plain view of Jesse Jackson and the audience. They remained there and attempted to stare me down for much of the meeting. A security guard also came down from the rear of the room in an attempt to remove me. When I stayed put, Jackson eventually told the man to leave us be.

Jesse Jackson was at the head table, no more that ten feet in front of us. He started making derogatory comments about me and other black conservatives. He said, "The issue is not conservatives or liberals. The issue is some parasites who want to pick up apples from trees they didn't shake." Jackson's reference to shaking a tree says a lot about the man and his motives. He admitted that he "shakes" corporate trees for millions—and he's been very successful at it.

Once the meeting was over, I got up and started to make my way to the exit. But Jonathan Jackson blocked my way out. He made insulting comments to me. I walked around him and proceeded to walk toward the exit. But the show wasn't over.

On my way out, I stopped at the refreshment table and sent Ermias over to give a business card and brochure to Irv Miller of Toyota. Miller was standing by the head table chatting with a few people.

When Ermias returned, we proceeded to walk toward the exit. Jonathan, accompanied by several others, came right toward me. He shoved me—really hard—and I told him that he was not allowed to touch me, not to put his hands on me.

At this point we were surrounded by at least a dozen of Jackson's associates. They were calling me "nigger" and taunting me with other racial slurs. Jonathan Jackson was making obscene remarks and gestures to me. Jesse was there the whole time, watching his son assault me, and did nothing to stop him. Judge Mathis was yelling at me too, saying, "Where's O'Reilly when you need him? You're always on his show."

I could hear Jesse Jackson in the background yelling, "Get his ass out of here."

As I was verbally abused and physically assaulted, I actually began fearing for my safety. I have had guns drawn on me in the past, but my experience with Jackson and his goon squad was something I'll never forget. For the first time in my life, I felt my life was really threatened.

Finally, another Jackson supporter yelled out to my assistant, Ermias, "You better get your boy out of here before he gets his ass kicked." Ermias put his arm around my chest and shoulder and pushed our way through the crowd. On our way out, we were followed by Jackson's people.

Jackson didn't allow any press to cover this meeting, but one of our BOND employees was recording the event. When he was discovered, Jackson's handlers removed him from the meeting. Later our employee was able to get a short interview with Jackson because his people still didn't know the man was from my organization.

As a result of these physical and verbal assaults against me, I contacted my friend Larry Klayman with Judicial Watch, and we have filed a lawsuit against Rainbow/PUSH, Jackson, Mathis, and Jonathan Jackson for assault, intentional infliction of emotional distress, and false imprisonment. Jonathan is also accused of battery, civil rights violations, and intentional interference with prospective economic advantage. Jackson's attempt to get my lawsuit against him and his associates dropped has failed. A California superior court refused Jackson's request for dismissal in April 2002, so the case can now move forward. As of this writing, we are awaiting trial and look to have a date very soon.

I realize that people like Jesse Jackson are evil. He has no respect for physical or spiritual laws. He may think he's going to silence me, but he will fail. Jackson needs to learn that he is not above the law, that he will not get away with his crimes, and that there will be serious consequences for his actions.

EXPOSING JACKSON'S SHAKEDOWN RACKET

Kenneth Timmerman is an investigative reporter for *Insight* magazine and has published a devastating exposé of Jesse Jackson's racket in a recent book. Timmerman's *Shakedown: Exposing the Real Jesse Jackson* is a must-read for any American—black, white, red, yellow, or brown—who wants to know the truth about Jesse Jackson's assault against our nation's corporations. Jackson has mastered the art of the shakedown by using the race card to frighten business leaders into handing his organization and his friends millions of dollars in funds, supposedly to help minorities.

Timmerman exposes the fact that "Reverend" Jackson is not really a properly ordained minister, that Jackson is lying when he claims that he held Dr. Martin Luther King Jr. in his arms after he'd been shot by an assassin in Memphis, and that in Chicago, he and his associates developed a cozy relationship with an extremely violent street gang known as the Blackstone Rangers, once headed by Jeff Fort.[2]

Jackson introduced his half brother, Noah Robinson, to Fort, and he, Robinson, and Fort began working together on various business deals in Chicago involving city contracts and other enterprises. Jeff Fort was eventually sent to jail for life in 1986 for a plot that netted him $2.5 million from Libya. He was planning on blowing up U.S. installations for Col. Moammar Gadhafi, the Libyan dictator.[3] Noah Robinson was arrested in 1988 and convicted of murder-for-hire, drug trafficking, and racketeering—the same year that Jackson was running for president of the United States.[4]

Unlike his friends, Jackson opted for more "legal" scams. Corporate leaders would much prefer to be shaken down for half a million dollars than to get involved in costly lawsuits, boycotts, and the bad publicity that Jackson can generate by calling CEOs racists. Timmerman told WorldNetDaily.com in an interview about his book, "I've had a number of CEOs come to me and say paying Jesse Jackson $400,000 or $500,000 was the price of doing business."[5]

Toyota is far from the only company who has given in to Jackson's racket. The list is long and includes major corporations such as Coca Cola, Boeing, AT&T, Anheuser-Busch, and Viacom.

This criminal shakedown will not stop until corporate leaders get up the courage to repudiate Jackson for what he is: a shakedown artist who is enriching himself by shaking the apple trees of corporate America.

This certainly requires courage. Years before Timmerman released *Shakedown*, a black reporter from Chicago named Barbara Reynolds wrote the first critical biography of Jackson and subsequently was run out of town and had to hire bodyguards after receiving death threats from Jackson's supporters. Timmerman told WOR (New York) radio's Bob Grant, "It really was on its way to becoming a best seller until Jesse and his friends intervened with the booksellers and everyone else. [They] got her kicked off the airwaves and basically, run out of Chicago."[6] Since Reynolds' experience, no other journalist until Timmerman has attempted to chronicle Jackson's exploits in book form.

According to Holman W. Jenkins in the *Wall Street Journal*, "Nobody has shaken the money tree of corporate America more vigorously or more successfully in favor of his constituents. In our misnamed melting pot no one has operated so successfully to produce gravy for an ethnic elite by insisting on discriminatory treatment."[7]

Jenkins notes that Jackson has been successful in shaking $58 million from Flagstar, owner of Denny's restaurants; $865 million from Texaco; and millions more from other corporations cowed by Jackson's screw-turning efforts.

As Jenkins writes, "All of these successes ride on his ability to command a spotlight and to motivate sympathizers, and they place him squarely in the tradition of Boss Tweed. He is charismatic, a glutton for attention, and untroubled by an excessive delicacy about the relationship between means and ends—in other words, a fit keeper of this particular flame." Jenkins was being nearly poetic in his description of a hustler who bullies corporations into paying his rich black friends millions of dollars so these corporations can avoid being labeled "racist." His rich buddies, of course, then donate millions to his nonprofit efforts or join his trade bureau. Jackson, like a Mafia don, is very good at what he does.

Patrick Reilly, the editor of the Capital Research Center's *Organization Trends* and *Foundation Watch* newsletters, published an extensive exposé on Jackson's shady financial empire in April 2001. Reilly notes that Jackson has established several different organizations that are used to shake money from corporate America. Among those are the Wall Street Project in New York, the LaSalle Street Project in Chicago, the Ninth Street Project in Cleveland, the Wall Street Project West in Los Angeles, and the Silicon Valley Project in San Jose.

All of these machines are run under Jackson's Citizenship Education Fund (CEF), which collects large tax-deductible donations from corporations pressured into giving him money.[8]

In 2000, Jackson's various organizations brought in $17 million. His income that year was around $430,000, including $120,000 from his organizations and $260,000, according to Jackson, from his show on CNN. (His CNN gig was cancelled after revelations surfaced about his mistress and "love child," details of which will come later in the chapter.) Other money comes from speaking and writing fees. The CEF and Rainbow/PUSH Coalition both pay for Jackson's traveling expenses at various times and his former chief financial officer Billy Owens admitted that more than $450,000 of Jackson's traveling expenses in 2000 was funded by the Democratic party for get-out-the-vote efforts![9]

Of course, as millions pour into his various enterprises, there appears to be very little accountability or accurate accounting taking place. TV talk show host Bill O'Reilly, of the Fox News show "The O'Reilly Factor," has been one of the few on-air personalities who has been attempting to get the IRS to audit Jackson's shady finances.

O'Reilly has pointed out, for example, that in 1998, Jackson's non-profit Rainbow/PUSH organization cited $1.2 million in travel expenses, but Jackson provided no receipts to account for the money on his Illinois tax returns. In 1982, the IRS reviewed Jackson's accounts and found $1 million unaccounted for. He was forced to repay $700,000 to the feds but did not get a penalty for failing to file accurate tax returns.[10]

Jackson continues to remain an untouchable by the IRS and by whites in general who fear a backlash from any public attack against Jackson.

One of the few corporate leaders to challenge Jesse Jackson's shakedown schemes is T. J. Rodgers, who runs Cypress Semiconductor in Silicon Valley. Rodgers, who is white, is fed up with Jesse Jackson's attempts to lean on the computer industry to enrich himself and his wealthy friends.

Rodgers expressed his disdain for Jackson in a 1999 *San Jose Mercury News* op-ed for which he interviewed several black leaders:

I asked Gerald Reynolds, an African-American and former president of the Washington-based Center for New Black Leadership, why CEOs are so deferential to Jackson. "It's simple," he told me. "Jesse Jackson is a race hustler who makes his living shaking down corporations. Whites would rather be accused of being a child molester than a racist. Jesse's got the power to make corporate chieftains cower.

In the piece, Rodgers also related a conversation he had with Hoover Institution scholar Shelby Steele:

"Martin Luther King told people they had to take on the responsibility—the risk—to gain their freedom," Steele told me. "Jesse Jackson tells them that they are weak, victims of prejudice that have no responsibility for their situation, and that they should rely on him to get the concessions that will improve their situation. In my opinion, that message of 'victimhood' is a bigger barrier to progress than prejudice itself."

Rodgers wrapped it up with a stinging indictment:

Once, the civil rights movement was led by a great American who stirred the conscience of a nation. Today, its most visible spokesman is a hustler who exploits white shame for his own financial and political ends.

It is a pity that T.J. Rodgers appears to be the only leader in corporate America who has the guts to stand up to Jackson's game. Where are other white leaders who will join in exposing and repudiating this racist con artist?

JACKSON'S LOVE AFFAIR WITH TYRANTS AND TERRORISTS

There is much more to the Jackson scam than dishonest gain. Jackson has had a long and strange love affair with various communist and Muslim tyrants throughout his career as a "civil rights leader." This seems odd since Jackson claims to be a preacher who believes in Jesus Christ. Why he would consort with murderous atheists and Muslim extremists is difficult to explain unless you realize that Jackson's entire life is simply one fraud after another.

In 1979, for example, Jackson visited the Middle East and paid a friendly visit to terrorist Yasser Arafat. After their meeting, Jackson described this murderer as "educated, urbane, reasonable. I think his commitment to justice is an absolute one."[11]

In 1984, he and his long-time advisor Jack O'Dell, who is a Communist party member, and Mary Tate of the U.S. Peace Council (a front for the KGB) paid a cordial visit to Syrian dictator Hafaz Assad. In 1984, Jackson also visited communist Cuba and described dictator Fidel Castro as "the most honest, courageous politician I have ever met." And during his visit to the University of Havana, Jackson reportedly shouted out "Long live Castro! Long live Che Guevara!" Guevara, of course, is the communist terrorist who was killed in Bolivia in 1967 for attempting to overthrow the government there.[12]

Jackson's odd connection to communist subversives was detailed in an article by WorldNetDaily editor-in-chief Joseph Farah in 2001. Farah points out the following about Jackson's close association with communists:

1. *Political Affairs,* the official journal of the Communist Party USA, noted in its January 1984 edition that, "Our '84 electoral activity began with the formation of Rainbow Coalition in Harlem in support of Jesse Jackson's campaign for the presidency."

2. Communist Party member Jack O'Dell has served as director of international affairs for the National Rainbow Coalition.

3. Gus Hall, the late leader of the Communist Party USA, endorsed Jackson for president in 1988.

4. In 1985, Jackson was a keynote speaker to celebrate the 10th anniversary of the communist takeover of Vietnam. The event was sponsored by the Communist Party.

5. Jackson was a speaker at a 1984 symposium sponsored by the *Marxist Black Scholar* magazine.[13]

All of these unsavory relationships make one wonder about the character of this self-proclaimed preacher. These relationships reveal the true nature and goals of Jackson—not his carefully spun media image as one who helps the downtrodden and is motivated by a concern for civil rights. Jackson appears to be sympathetic to Marxist causes as well as Islamic causes that will undermine international stability and lead to more war and strife. It will lead to the institution of dictatorships (or the strengthening of existing ones) over millions in the Middle East and Africa.

For a man who claims to hold the mantle of Dr. Martin Luther King Jr., a visionary who dreamed of freedom for his people, Jackson seems strangely fond of slavery.

JACKSON FATHERS A "LOVE CHILD"

Although the *National Enquirer* is usually associated with unethical or flawed journalism, this scandal rag got it right in its January 30, 2001, issue. The headline reads: "Jesse Jackson's Love Child—His 38-year marriage blows up over secret family. He even took pregnant mistress to meet Clinton in Oval Office."

The article then details the fact that Jackson had maintained a secret four-year adulterous affair with his former aide, Karin Stanford. She had given birth to his baby on May 1, 1999. The story says he had been secretly paying her about $10,000 a month after DNA tests proved that he was the father.

Stanford told the *Enquirer* that she had received a payment of $40,000 before taking maternity leave from her job as the director of Jackson's Rainbow Coalition office in Washington D.C. She quietly relocated from Washington to Los Angeles, where she continued to work as a part-time researcher for Jackson's organization. The *Enquirer* noted that she had purchased a $365,000 home in a quiet Los Angeles neighborhood.

Connie Chung interviewed Stanford in August 2001. Stanford told Chung that she had gone to court to make sure she would continue to get $4,000 a month in child support payments from Jackson. He had asked her to sign a confidentiality agreement, and she refused. She admitted that it didn't matter to her that Jackson was already married and had five children. She told Chung, "From what I understood about Rev. Jackson's marriage was that it was basically a political marriage."[14]

Two talk show hosts on CNN then began to spread the falsehood that Stanford was a "stalker" of Jesse Jackson because she had gone public with her revelations of his "love child." This same tactic was used by Clinton supporters against Kathleen Willey, Gennifer Flowers, Juanita Broaddrick, and other women who accused Clinton of sexual misconduct. The goal is always to vilify the victim of sexual exploitation and justify the perpetrator's actions—but only if he's a certified liberal.

On CNN's "Talk Back Live" program in August 2001, Tavis Smiley brought up the issue of so-called "political stalking"—referring to Stanford as a stalker. Smiley then asked associate and guest Tom Joyner, "Do you think there's any credence to this notion that Jesse Jackson is being politically stalked either by the media or by the mother [Stanford] in this case?"

Joyner replied, "I think he is stalked by both. And I think it is pretty evident that he is. And it is a shame that the child is being used, is being exploited . . . for someone else's agenda, be it the mother or be it the media. But this child is being exploited."[15]

Moments later, Stanford called in and began berating them for suggesting that she was a political stalker. She told these liberal hosts that she'd tried to get formal agreements from Jackson that he would provide for his child's education but that he had refused to do so. She also made an interesting comment: "Not one African-American media organization reached out to me to ask me a question. What you guys seem to do is print Reverend Jackson's statements, his perspective, without asking me. Most of the other news organizations would at least try to get two sides to the story before they go on the national TV and start calling me a stalker, because I'm just not that."[16]

After I watched Karin Stanford talk about her situation with Jackson on ABC's "20/20" that August, I issued a press release calling upon Jackson to stop calling himself a preacher. Jackson's exposure as an adulterer once again shows what a hypocritical fraud he is. In the press release, I said, "This man is in favor of killing other people's unborn babies but not his own. He counsels Bill Clinton about his affair with Monica Lewinsky and brings his pregnant mistress. And he says he won't appear on a TV show because the media will hurt the child. It's being without a father that will cause the damage.

"And he has the gall to continue calling himself 'Reverend'! Now is the time to stand on moral principle and demand that Jackson drop the title 'Reverend' and speak out against this immoral man."

BOND'S NATIONAL DAY OF REPUDIATION OF JESSE JACKSON

With a track record like his, it is amazing Jackson is still around and as popular as he is. He has been coddled by a compliant liberal media and fawned over by leftist talk show hosts who still pay homage to him—in spite of his adultery, financial mismanagement, and obvious efforts to exploit racial tensions wherever he can find them.

Jackson has also been protected by liberal politicians—such as those within the Congressional Black Caucus. The IRS has largely kept a hands-off policy when it comes to Jackson's confusing business arrangements and nonprofit organizations. And, in my view, the state of Illinois is still giving Jackson a "Get out of Jail Free" card to continue his practice of not itemizing consulting or travel expenses on his tax returns.[17]

Jesse Jackson is a disgrace to his race and I am curious about his political loyalties. Are they to the United States or some other foreign power or political ideology that is a threat to the security of America? He seems to be more comfortable in the company of communists, extremist politicians, and murderous street gang leaders than with any other religious or social groups. You say a lot about who you are by the company you keep.

Jesse Jackson is a major player in reversing our nation's civil rights gains over the past forty years. By either creating or exploiting racial tensions, he is continually adding fuel to a racial fire. Racism is largely a thing of the past—yet if you're Jesse Jackson, racism is your bread and butter and your ticket to power and millions of dollars.

For all these reasons, for more than a dozen years now, I have been calling upon Americans of all ethnic backgrounds and religious beliefs to rise up to repudiate Jesse Jackson. Four years ago, we took it up a notch. BOND held its first "National Day of Repudiation of Jesse Jackson" on January 17, 2000, at the Federal Building in Westwood, California. I was joined in this protest by Ezola Foster; Joyce Smith, head of Rejoice Ministries in Houston, Texas; talk show host Bob Enyart; and Baptist preacher Dr. Wiley Drake of the First Southern Baptist Church of Buena Park.

In my prepared remarks I vowed that I would hold a national day of repudiation against Jackson every year until he repents of his ways and stops attempting to tear the races apart for his own personal gain. I believe Dr. King is turning over in his grave seeing what has become of his movement due to the likes of Jackson.

I told those gathered for this event that Jesse Jackson is nothing more than David Duke in black skin.

This first National Day of Repudiation came in the wake of one of Jackson's frequent efforts to create racial hatred. The incident in Decatur, Illinois, at a high school football game was still being talked about in the press. As you may recall, six black MacArthur High School students were expelled after going on a rampage through the crowd, hitting students and knocking people over.

The school, of course, did the right thing by expelling them. They were unruly hooligans. Jesse Jackson—always ready to exaggerate any racial incident—immediately descended on the town and started crying "racism" against school authorities. After organizing the usual rent-a-mob, Jackson and more than two thousand angry protesters marched through the streets of Decatur, demanding that the students' one-year suspension be cut further.

Jackson was once again exposed for what he is: a cold, selfish manipulator. Time and again he lies in wait, only to spring up when he can inflame a racial situation. He doesn't care a bit about the thugs he was protecting or the rest of the students at the high school. This is just how Jackson operates.

At our second National Day of Repudiation of Jesse Jackson, in January 2001, we had just gone through a horrendous battle in Florida over dimpled chads. Jackson had done his best to create racial unrest in Florida. He made false claims that Republicans had intimidated black voters and demanded a federal investigation. He also made national headlines by leading protests against the election of George W. Bush as our president, and he accused the U.S. Supreme Court of engineering a coup d'etat.

At our third Repudiation Day, in 2002, a group of radical leftist Mexicans showed up to counter-protest. They were intent on creating a violent confrontation, but we didn't take the bait and fortunately no one was injured. For a man who claims to be a "Reverend" and man of God, Jackson certainly has some dangerous and violent friends.

We held our fourth National Day of Repudiation in January of 2003 in front of Jackson's Rainbow/PUSH office in Cecil Murray's FAME Renaissance Center building in South Central Los Angeles. Joining me in this protest were talk show host and WorldNetDaily.com columnist Jane Chastain, activist Ted Hayes, Pastor Drake, and Rabbi Nachum Shifren. Imagine—men and women, black and white, gentile and Jew, all together for a great cause. This is the *real* rainbow coalition!

During each of these days of repudiation, we say the Pledge of Allegiance, sing the National Anthem, and have one of our young men or women from BOND read portions of Dr. King's "I Have A Dream" speech.

In my presentation, I noted, "The purpose of this event is to show the contrast between Dr. King's dream and Jesse Jackson's nightmare. Jackson has hijacked Dr. King's dream; as a result, black Americans are suffering under his 'leadership,' and we're going to repudiate him until he repents and apologizes to black Americans."[18]

I chose to hold this event on Dr. King's birthday because Jackson is the antithesis of what Dr. King stood for in the early years of his work on behalf of blacks. I am still inspired by the truths he expressed in his "I Have A Dream" speech on the Capitol Hill Mall in 1963.

All Americans should take time to reread his compelling words because they express what I feel and what many other blacks feel about this nation and the importance of racial harmony.

Here are just a few of Dr. King's words. Notice how they contrast with the black racism espoused by the Afrocentrists, Congressional Black Caucus, NAACP, Jackson, and other racial agitators:

- We must forever conduct our struggle on the high plane of dignity and discipline. We must not allow our creative protest to degenerate into physical violence. Again and again we must rise to the majestic heights of meeting physical violence with soul force. The marvelous new militancy which has engulfed the Negro community must not lead us to distrust of all white people, for many of our white brothers, as evidenced by their presence here today, have come to realize that their destiny is tied up with our destiny and their freedom is inextricably bound to our freedom. We cannot walk alone.

- I have a dream that one day this nation will rise up and live out the true meaning of its creed: "We hold these truths to be self-evident: that all men are created equal."

- I have a dream that my four children will one day live in a nation where they will not be judged by the color of their skin but by the content of their character.

- When we let freedom ring, when we let it ring from every village and every hamlet, from every state and every city, we will be able to speed up that day when all of God's children, black men and white men, Jews and Gentiles, Protestants and Catholics, will be able to join hands and sing in the words of the old Negro spiritual, "Free at last! Free at last! Thank God Almighty, we are free at last!"

Dr. King had a dream. He was seeking racial harmony and equality under the law. He was seeking a colorblind society where blacks were judged by their character, not by the color of their skin. Jesse Jackson and his Afrocentrist allies, however, want just the opposite. They have a nightmare, not a dream. The shade of a person's skin is now the *primary* way that individuals are being judged—and it determines what kind of special treatment they'll receive. Being black is a ticket to privilege, federal grants, and special consideration in applying to college.

GOOD NEWS ON JACKSON'S EMPIRE

There are signs that Jackson's corrupt racist empire may be slowly but surely collapsing. The revelations about Jackson's adulterous relationship and the fostering of an out-of-wedlock child have apparently given some businessmen and women and even black religious leaders courage to withdraw support from Jackson.

News reports in early January 2002 indicated that his organizations had shrunk from one hundred employees in 2001 to fewer than fifty in 2002. Rainbow/PUSH, the Wall Street Project, and the Citizenship Education Fund have all been downsized. One banker, who wished to remain anonymous, told Cybercast News Service (CNS), "His money is drying up, the Wall Street Project is tanking. He is reeling."[19]

Wall Street executives are also beginning to question Jackson's patriotism and loyalty to America after hearing some of his inflammatory comments made after the September 11, 2001, terrorist attack on America. Jackson opposed the U.S. bombing campaign in Afghanistan and called U.S. Attorney General John Ashcroft a "terrorist suspect" who supposedly threatens democracy.[20]

In Ken Timmerman's book, *Shakedown,* he notes that after the 9-11 attack on our nation, Jackson showed little concern for the worst national tragedy since Pearl Harbor. Timmerman told Cybercast News Service:

> When the entire country is in a state of grief and patriotic resurgence, he wasn't flying [the flag] at his home. It wasn't on his car, it wasn't on his lapel, it wasn't on stage behind him. In front of the cameras, there wasn't visible a flag in the whole place. There was no sense or

expression of either mourning of grief or even of sympathy for the victims of September 11th.[21]

In addition to losing credibility and finances, Jackson lost power in the executive branch after the election of President Bush. But he still has powerful friends in the Congressional Black Caucus who can be expected to shill for him.

WE MUST ALL REPUDIATE JACKSON!

Americans of all races and colors must rise up and repudiate Jesse Jackson as the spokesman for blacks. No one elected him to speak for us, we don't want him speaking for us, and he is an embarrassment to us. Further, no one person speaks for blacks any more than one person speaks for whites or Hispanics.

The whole idea of racial groups having a leader or leaders is ridiculous. Yet religious and political demagogues have conned us into believing that these corrupt and un-elected black spokesmen somehow represent the real interests of all blacks. They don't. In fact, they only represent their own political and financial interests. They are really harming racial relations because whites and other ethnic groups automatically see the corruption of hustlers like Jesse Jackson as representative of the entire black race.

To paraphrase the words of Dr. Martin Luther King, "We shall overcome Jesse Jackson."

8

Louis Farrakhan, American Hitler

—⁓—

The rise of America's biggest bigot

In October 1995, I watched as hundreds of thousands of weak black men attended Louis Farrakhan's Million Man March in Washington, D.C.

Farrakhan has risen to fame under the guise of wanting to help black men take charge of their lives and the lives of their families. The "minister" entices his listeners by giving them a little truth about history and about slavery in America. Once they are emotionally involved with Farrakhan's version of "truth," he then reveals his true motive, which is to blame the white man (especially Jews) for everything. All the reasons blacks can't make it, all of their problems, are due to the "blue-eyed devil," the white man in America.

The Jew, according to Farrakhan, comes into the black community, takes all of their money, and brings it back to his own community, thereby exploiting blacks. Do people realize that it is normal for a business person to "set up shop" wherever possible, to earn a living, and to take his or her profits back to wherever he or she wishes? Is there a law that says a person must spend his or her earnings in a particular area? After hearing this theme repeated over and over, blacks are blaming not only Jews but also Koreans and Hispanics. Should we be surprised to learn that a year before the Rodney King riots in Los Angeles, emissaries of Farrakhan's Nation of Islam had come into town to preach hatred against Korean businessmen as exploiters of blacks?[1]

These prejudice-filled blacks should admit that they are jealous of the ingenuity of these people who so easily set up businesses and earn a living when blacks, by and large, are not able to do so themselves. Instead of spending so much energy hating merchants and businessmen, of whatever race or background, blacks should try to learn from them and put their principles into practice. If this were done, blacks would achieve the same standard of living as any other race. It is this motivation to justify weakness that Louis Farrakhan uses to confuse and confound people in order to get them under his own authority.

Some folks say Farrakhan is a godly man, a man sent by God. They also say that Farrakhan preaches self-reliance. Well, so did Adolf Hitler. History tells us that Hitler invoked the name of God and used "truth," which he perverted, to get control of the German people. Once Hitler got their allegiance, he was able to convince them of almost anything. He persuaded them to give up their weapons, and then the atrocities—too brutal to describe—began. The rest is history.

In my opinion, Farrakhan rose to near-Hitler status that fateful day in October of 1995 on the National Mall in Washington D.C. And we, the American people, are going to live to regret it. The power that Farrakhan gained that day in our nation's capital will be too much for the American people to handle. It will be worse than the outcome of the O.J. Simpson trial in serving to separate the races and to bring hatred into the hearts and minds of black people.

Before this march, many blacks viewed Louis Farrakhan as a teacher of hate and a manipulator of discord. But now, many of these same people are convinced that Farrakhan is a strong black man who loves black people and who has their best interests at heart. This also includes so-called Christians who used to be quite leery and suspect of black Muslim ministers and their teachings. Now these "Christians" have been very much converted by Louis Farrakhan.

The status Louis Farrakhan gained the day of the Million Man March has been parlayed into a position which allows him to meet with evil world leaders like Moammar Gadhafi. Meetings like this can only be taking place for one reason—to unify the worldwide militant Muslim movement. To what end? Does anyone really think this man's ultimate aims are peaceful? It's obvious to me that the Nation of Islam has always been a subversive and violent organization.

BIZARRE RELIGIOUS BELIEFS AND DANGEROUS GOALS

The Nation of Islam began in the summer of 1930 when a man calling himself Wallace Farad Muhammad arrived in Detroit. He claimed he had just come from Mecca with a mission to teach blacks the truth about the white race. He taught blacks to prepare for the battle of Armageddon, which he claimed was to be the final confrontation between blacks and whites. Blacks would win this battle and take over the world.[2]

Muhammad began to gather a large following with his preaching of this basic belief system: Allah is the one supreme God, the white man is the devil, and blacks are the cream of planet earth. From 1930 to 1933, he recruited eight thousand followers.

One of these followers was an unemployed auto worker named Elijah Poole. Poole was the son of a Baptist preacher/sharecropper who had grown up in Georgia. Poole became a fanatical follower of Muhammad and rose quickly within the ranks. He changed his name to Elijah Muhammad and became the chief minister in the Nation of Islam.

In June of 1934, Wallace Farad Muhammad mysteriously disappeared from Detroit and Elijah Muhammad became the head of the Nation of Islam—a position he held for more than forty years.

Wallace Farad Muhammad passed his strange theology along to Elijah Muhammad, and these beliefs have remained fairly consistent up to the present day. The theology of the Nation consists of the following:

1. In addition to Allah, there are many lesser gods, and these gods are actually men. Elijah Muhammad, for example, taught that Wallace Farad Muhammad was one of these gods. These gods are also subject to death.

2. The universe began 78 trillion years ago when a black god created himself from a single atom, which formed itself out of nothing. According to Elijah Muhammad, "He was the only One in the whole entire dark Universe. He had to wait until the atom of life produced brains to think what He needed. How long was that? I don't know, Brothers. But He was a Black man, a Black man!" For the past 66 trillion years, the universe has been run by a council of 24 black gods.

3. One of these black gods, named Yakub, became evil and created the white race only 6,000 years ago. He created this white race by allowing only light-skinned blacks to mate and by killing all black babies. He died after 150 years, but his evil successors continued his experiment, which lasted more than 600 years, on the Isle of Patmos. His followers eventually produced the white race. In this process, they removed morality and decency from the white man. When the white race eventually left Patmos, they began to wage war against all other races on the planet. At some point during this early history of the white race, some of them tried to change back into black men by reverse breeding. This is how gorillas and monkeys came to exist.

4. The white race was allowed by the black council of gods to rule the earth for only 6,000 years. This period supposedly ended in 1914, but Elijah Muhammad taught that the council extended the deadline in order to allow more time for the black man to rise up. Muhammad taught that once the black man had awakened to his

true nature and purpose, he would remove the white man from the face of the earth in a final battle. Muhammad wrote, "The Black man is the true owner of the earth. Now the God of Justice Has Risen up to Deliver the rule back to the Black Man and give him a place in the sun that justifies his ownership."

5. There is no life after death or concept of salvation in Nation of Islam theology. "Salvation" consists only in adhering to the teachings of Farrakhan and Elijah Muhammad.[3]

These five points sum up some of the bizarre beliefs that energize members of the Nation of Islam—and which guide Louis Farrakhan to this day.

Muhammad hated America and loved its enemies. When the Japanese bombed Pearl Harbor in 1941, Elijah Muhammad rejoiced and refused to register for the draft. He was sent to prison for three years and got out in 1946, resuming leadership of the Nation of Islam. The FBI was so distrustful of Muhammad and his activities that it carefully monitored him for decades, especially as he eventually developed a close relationship with Fidel Castro and Marxist dictators in Africa.[4]

Muhammad was also a serial adulterer who frequently had as many as seven different adulterous relationships going on at the same time. Through these adulteries, he sired thirteen children. FBI surveillance tapes reveal Muhammad telling these women that they were the beneficiaries of his "divine seed" and lying about his intentions to marry them.[5]

MALCOLM X AND LOUIS FARRAKHAN

Malcolm X, who has been immortalized in film and through his book, *The Autobiography of Malcolm X*, joined the Nation of Islam in 1948 and quickly became a major force within the movement.

His autobiography describes his eventual disillusionment with Muhammad after learning of his leader's adulterous relationships. He also traveled to Mecca and realized that Muslims came in all colors—including white. His hatred of whites diminished over time as a result of this trip.

Malcolm X had been a mentor to Louis Farrakhan, who eventually replaced him as head of a Harlem Nation of Islam Temple. Malcolm X became viewed as a traitor to the Nation for openly discussing Muhammad's adulterous affairs and for rejecting racism. Malcolm X began calling Muhammad a racist and a phony; the Nation's "god" didn't appreciate the criticism. Upon learning of Malcolm X's betrayal, Muhammad told his followers, "It's time to close that nigger's eyes."[6]

In December 1964, Louis Farrakhan wrote an article for a Nation newspaper, *Muhammad Speaks* stating that Malcolm X "was worthy of death." Two months later, three black Muslim assassins approached Malcolm X while he was giving a lecture at Manhattan's Audubon Ballroom, shooting him fifteen to sixteen times and killing him.[7]

One of the men convicted of the killing was Muhammad Abdul Aziz, who spent 19 years in jail for his role in the assassination. Interestingly enough, in 1998, Louis Farrakhan hired Aziz to be the new head of Mosque No. 7 in New York City. Aziz was also made Farrakhan's regional security chief for the East Coast and was given the job of reviving the Fruit of Islam paramilitary arm of the Nation.[8]

When Elijah Muhammad died in 1975, his son Warith Deen Muhammad took over as head of the Nation of Islam. He began changing the Nation's theology to conform more closely to the teachings of Islam, and he changed the name of the group to the World Community of Islam. Later, he changed its name to the American Muslim Mission. Muhammad eventually disbanded the group altogether, and his followers were absorbed into the Islamic movement.

Louis Farrakhan resurrected the Nation of Islam in 1978 and reinstated its security force, a paramilitary group that is frequently staffed by former prisoners. Since 1999, the Nation of Islam has managed to get an estimated $20 million from the federal government to provide security services for public housing projects throughout the United States. The Fruit of Islam guards have provided security for these projects in Chicago, Los Angeles, Pittsburgh, Washington, and other cities. The efforts of the Nation in public housing projects serve as an excellent way of recruiting new haters into the movement.[9]

FARRAKHAN'S CLOSE ENCOUNTER OF THE THIRD KIND

Farrakhan claims to receive instructions for running the Nation of Islam from the spirit of Elijah Muhammad. On October 24, 1989, Farrakhan gave a speech at a press conference at the J.W. Marriott Hotel in Washington D.C., in which he described a vision he had of an encounter with Elijah Muhammad inside a flying saucer on a mountaintop near the town of Tepotzlan, Mexico.

This close encounter supposedly took place in 1985. Farrakhan says he was invited to enter the flying saucer, which he describes as a "Wheel," which transported him higher into the sky to link up with the "Mother Wheel." He claims that once inside the Mother Wheel, he began hearing the dead Elijah Muhammad speaking to him and giving him updates on international politics and what role he was to play in linking arms with black racists and Islamic radicals throughout the world.

According to Muhammad, Farrakhan had a job to complete on earth, and once he had accomplished it, he would be allowed to return to the Mother Wheel for a face-to-face meeting with Muhammad.

Farrakhan's belief in UFOs is not new to Nation of Islam theology. Muhammad taught that this "Mother Wheel" had existed for more than sixty years. Writing in "Message to the Black Man," Muhammad states:

The present wheel-shaped plane known as the Mother of Planes, is one-half mile by a half mile and is the largest mechanical man-made object in the sky. It is a small human planet made for the purpose of destroying the present world of the enemies of Allah. The cost to build such a plane is staggering. The finest brains were used to build it. It is

capable of staying in outer space six to twelve months at a time without coming into the earth's gravity. It carried fifteen hundred bombing
planes with the most deadliest explosives—the type used in bringing up
mountains on the earth. The very same method is to be used in the
destruction of this world.[10]

Farrakhan claims that the dead Elijah Muhammad had warned him
that President Reagan was planning a war and that he was to hold a
press conference to warn Americans about this war. After the vision
faded, Farrakhan says he realized that the war was going to be against
his friend, Libyan dictator Moammar Gadhafi. As a result of this
vision, he says he joined forces with the All African Peoples
Revolutionary party and fifteen other groups of blacks, Native
Americans, Hispanics, and whites to oppose any attack on Libya.

At his press conference in 1989, Farrakhan claimed that the job he
had been given to do by Muhammad was to warn blacks that President
George H. W. Bush and his administration were planning a war against
blacks: "I am here to announce today that President Bush has met with
his Joint Chiefs of Staff, under the direction of Colin Powell, to plan a
war against the black people of America, the Nation of Islam and
Louis Farrakhan, with particular emphasis on our Black youth, under
the guise of a war against drug sellers, drug users, gangs, and violence—all under the head of national security."[11]

In 1996, Farrakhan embarked on a "World Friendship Tour,"
which included stops in five nations described by the U.S. government
as sponsors of state terrorism: Libya, Iran, Iraq, Sudan, and Syria.
During this tour, it was reported that Farrakhan repeatedly denounced
the U.S., calling it the "Great Satan" while in Iran.[12]

During Farrakhan's visit to Libya, Gadhafi pledged $1 billion
to encourage minority political action in the U.S. According to Gadhafi,
"American blacks could set up their own state within the United States
with the largest black army in the world." Gadhafi also noted about
Libya, "Our confrontation with America used to be like confronting a
fortress from outside. Today, we have found a loophole to enter the
fortress and to confront it from within."[13]

Of course, Louis Farrakhan was the "loophole" Gadhafi was referring to. Farrakhan recruits many of his hateful followers from our nation's prisons. These individuals already have a problem with authority, are predisposed to engage in violent acts, and constitute a ready-made military force. This force can subvert our nation with hundreds of terrorist acts when directed to do so by Farrakhan.

FARRAKHAN, THE BELTWAY SNIPERS, AND THE FIVE PERCENTERS

The arrest of Beltway snipers John Muhammad and John Lee Malvo by law enforcement authorities in Maryland in October 2002 revealed a frightening linkage between Farrakhan and the alleged killers.

As police learned more about John Muhammad, they began connecting the dots between this killer and the Nation of Islam. Muhammad was a security guard for Farrakhan during his 1995 "Million Man March" in Washington D.C. Muhammad had also been inspired to action by the September 11, 2001, terrorist attack upon our nation and was known to have made anti-American statements to his friends when he lived in Washington state.[14]

The racial and political hatred that Muhammad and Malvo had for the United States was also apparently linked to a little known offshoot of the Nation known as the "Five Percenters." Neither the Nation of Islam nor the Five Percenters have been implicated in these shootings.

The link between the Beltway snipers and the Five Percenters was noted in an Associated Press report on October 26, 2002. AP reported on the contents of the sniper letter that was left behind by the killers on a tree behind a steakhouse in Ashland, Virginia. The letter contained numerous clues to the identity and religious beliefs of the killers. The letter referred to the author as "God." It also included the phrase "word is bond," a statement used by "The Nation of Gods and Earths," another name for Five Percenters. The headquarters of this group is the Allah School in Mecca, located in New York City.[15]

The Five Percenters believe that the black man is "God" and

women are to be called "Earth." They also believe that they are the five percent of the population who are truly righteous and understand spiritual truths. Five Percenters say that blacks are the original people of the earth, that they created civilization, and that whites ("devils") have deceived the world, causing people to worship false gods. A number of hip-hop artists have been influenced by the Five Percenters, including Public Enemy, Ice Cube, Gang Starr, and others.

One hip hop group, Sunz of Man, is blunt in its lyrics about its Five Percenter goals. In "Can I See You," they rap: "[C]arry .45s in these last days and times . . . [A]n original black man with a plan to run these devils off my motherf—-ing land." Ominously, Public Enemy rapper Chuck D has called hip hop music "the black CNN."[16]

Law enforcement officials are deeply concerned about the influence that the Five Percenters are having in our nation's prisons as they recruit members into their "religion." In essence, these groups are simply gangs of anti-white, anti-American racists who believe that a coming race war between blacks and whites will result in a black victory.

I consider Louis Farrakhan to be a serious threat to our national security and a subversive influence in our society. It is his theological belief that a race war is inevitable and that blacks will emerge victorious. He has political alignments with some of the world's most infamous terrorists, and his Nation of Islam is nothing less than an anti-American army that is poised to help destroy our nation.

I believe that if people do not wake up, and soon, we *will* have a race war in America—one that will cause bloodshed on a scale that we have never seen before. In my speaking to and interacting with many blacks, it is surprising to see the number of people who have actually bought into the views of this evil man. And their loyalty appears so strong they seem willing to do whatever Farrakhan bids, which is very frightening.

Yet our nation's black preachers continue to ally themselves with this American Hitler. Their mutual hatred of whites and America is what links them together in their common cause against our nation.

If a man teaches hate, he is your enemy. At the Million Man March and rally, I heard many speeches by those who were not friends of the black family and the black community. We have already lost two generations of blacks to gangs, dope, promiscuity, teenage parenthood, truancy, welfare dependence, and crime in large part due to this evil, defeatist, "We are the victims of racism by whites/Jews" philosophy. If we do not wake up, we are going to lose our entire country.

We must wake up so that we can see the enemy wherever the enemy is—regardless of race or color. There was a time that I, too, was under the spell of this type of black leader. I have come to understand that our problems are not between races, but between good and evil. And good and evil can come from any person. Until we become aware of this and learn to know ourselves, we will not be able to see that.

If we cannot see error and wrong in a person without regard to race or color, then our enemy will be seen as a friend, and a true friend will be viewed as an enemy. That is now taking place in the black community. Black people tell each other that a black should not criticize a fellow black in the company of whites. Those blacks who do have clear vision and state the truth plainly are called "sellouts," "traitors to the cause," or "Uncle Toms."

We have been made to feel guilty if we dare to disagree with black ministers of whatever stripe. Somehow we've been convinced that even God will punish us if we question ministers and these black "leaders." This is a very successful strategy to control blacks and keep them in line. Without scrutiny or criticism, the leaders can remain leaders and continue to get away with their lies.

This method of deception that has served to keep us confused victims has been in existence in the black community for the past forty years—entirely too long. I believe God wants us to question our leaders as well as ourselves. I believe these people are false prophets, hypocrites, bags of bones, and deceivers. These "leaders" know the truth, but they will not tell it to the black community because they want to keep this community in ignorance for their own personal power and gain.

9

Al Sharpton, Riot King

—ɯ—

Blacks need to reexamine this Jesse Jackson wannabe

His star is rising these days. He's regularly on TV. He's recently authored a book. His aspirations for the U.S. presidency are well known and discussed. He is the only prominent black "leader" poised to eclipse both Jesse Jackson and Louis Farrakhan.

Al Sharpton supposedly began preaching when he was four years old and was ordained as a Pentecostal minister at the age of nine. He preached on a tour with gospel legend Mahalia Jackson.

That same year, 1964, Sharpton's parents split up because of his father's incestuous relationship with Al's half sister, which produced a child. The boy was Al's brother and nephew. Sharpton wrote of his father's affair in his 1996 autobiography, *Go and Tell Pharaoh*, "I had to watch my mother, whom I loved more than anyone, live with the fact that her daughter had stolen her husband and that the two of them had given life of [sic] a child, out of wedlock. To this day, I don't know how [my mother] lived with the humiliation."[1]

The shock of this occurrence on the mind of young Al Sharpton must have been tremendous and, looking at his subsequent shameless behavior as an adult, it must have had a major effect on his heart and mind.

At fourteen, he was given a job by Jesse Jackson as the director of the Southern Christian Leadership Conference's "Operation Breadbasket" effort.

Later, Sharpton met singer James Brown, and in his late teens he spent eighteen months on tour with Brown. The singer's oldest son, Teddy, had been killed in a car crash, and Brown began referring to the fiery young preacher as "my surrogate son." Sharpton's wife was one of Brown's backup singers, and Sharpton introduced Brown to his third wife. (If nothing else, the Brown-Sharpton connection could explain Sharpton's hair!)

Interestingly enough, James Brown has shown disdain for the whole idea of black leaders over the years: "That was all right when we didn't have the nerve and the ambition, but now you can be anything you want to be. *So you're your own leaders*," he said recently. Asked if he'd endorse Sharpton for president, he carefully said, "I would endorse his *intent*."[2]

ON THE MAKE

Sharpton first made national headlines in the 1980s when he involved himself in a number of racially charged incidents in various New York City neighborhoods, including the Bernard Goetz case (the "white subway shooter").

But he is most famous for his shameful involvement in a hoax perpetrated by a young black teenager named Tawana Brawley. In this 1987 case, Brawley claimed to have been kidnapped and raped by several white men. Sharpton wanted an opportunity to get his name in the press, and Brawley was his ticket. During the ensuing media frenzy, Sharpton accused a local prosecutor, Steven Pagones, of taking part in the raping of this girl.

As investigators looked into Brawley's alleged kidnapping and rape, they eventually determined that she had fabricated the story. Pagones sued Sharpton over falsely accusing him of participating in this alleged rape. In 1998, Pagones won a $345,000 judgment against Sharpton and two of his advisers. He had originally asked for a $395 million judgment. To this day, Sharpton has not apologized or indicated any remorse for publicly smearing Pagones.

Regarding the case, Sharpton wrote, "At some point the Brawley case stopped being about Tawana, and started being about me defending my mother and all the black women no one would fight for. I was not going to run away from her like my father had run away from my mother."[3]

This was Sharpton's way of rationalizing his outrageous behavior in the case.

What is less well known about Sharpton, however, is the role he played in the 1991 riot and resultant killing of a Jewish man in Crown Heights, New York. The riot was triggered when a Hasidic Jew was driving, accidentally jumped a curb, and killed a seven-year-old black boy. Immediately, Sharpton got involved and led protests in Crown Heights for four nights in a row. These protests consisted of hundreds of bottle-throwing drunks terrorizing what is normally a quiet Jewish neighborhood. During his speeches to his rioters, he referred to Jews as "diamond merchants" and his followers shouted, "kill the Jews."[4] At one point during these nightly riots, a group of fifteen of Sharpton's followers spotted Yankel Rosenbaum, a rabbinical student from Australia. Yelling "get the Jew," the mob cornered him, beat him, and stabbed him to death. (Although Sharpton did not urge the protesters to kill Rosenbaum, he was responsible for organizing this volatile protest.)

Sharpton has also been involved in other provocations to violence against Jews in New York. In 1995, his National Action Network led a two-month long protest outside of Freddy's Fashion Mart in Harlem. Freddy's Fashion Mart was a Harlem boutique owned by Freddy Harari, a Jew. Harari rented space in a building which was owned by a black church, the United House of Prayer, which owns much property in Harlem. In 1995, the building's owners decided to raise the rents on the business tenants. The raise in rent caused Harari to raise the rent on his subtenant, a black-owned music store. A dispute ensued. Al Sharpton decided to protest—not by criticizing the black landlords of the building, but by loudly denouncing the Jewish owner of Freddy's Fashion Mart. "We will not stand by," Sharpton warned, "and allow them to move this brother so that some white interloper can expand his business." Sharpton's National Action Network set up picket lines; customers going into Freddy's were spat upon and cursed as "traitors" and "Uncle Toms." Some protesters shouted, "Burn the Jew store down!" and simulated striking a match. "We're going to see that this cracker suffers," said Sharpton's colleague Morris Powell. On December 8, one of the protesters burst into Freddy's, shot four employees point-blank, then set the store on fire. Seven employees died in the inferno.[5]

Boston Globe columnist Jeff Jacoby originally reported on this hate-filled event spurred on by Al Sharpton in his December 14, 1995, column. He wondered why such ugly demonstrations were allowed to go on day after day without some response from law enforcement officials. Wrote Jacoby:

> We live now in the Age of Farrakhan, and the rules are clear. Some kinds of racial terror will be fought with unsleeping vigilance; others will be discreetly overlooked. Some hatemongers will be reviled and shunned; others will lead Million Man Marches. Some vitriolic threats will be met with every weapon at society's command. Others—'Burn the Jew store down' for instance—won't even be heard. Not until seven victims have been incinerated.[6]

Sharpton is not only the promoter of hatred against Jews; there is FBI-videotaped evidence that strongly links him to involvement with the Mafia in New York. In March of 1983, "Reverend" Al was caught by an FBI surveillance camera discussing a cocaine purchase with a man named Victor Quintana, who posed as a Latin American businessman. Quintana was an undercover FBI agent who was working on a case dealing with corruption in the boxing industry, which included Don King.

This videotape was aired in July 2002 on HBO's "Real Sports with Bryant Gumbel." In the tape, Sharpton is wearing a cowboy hat and talking about buying cocaine from Quintana. He insists, however, that he would have to run the deal by an unnamed boss. The *New York Daily News* reported in July 2002 that two sources close to this 1983 investigation said that Sharpton's unnamed boss was Daniel Pagano, a member of the Genovese crime family, which had links to the recording industry. Pagano and Sharpton were long-time friends.[7]

News reports indicate that when Sharpton was confronted with the videotape by FBI agents, he decided to become an informant for the FBI against Pagano. The Mafia hoodlum was eventually indicted on racketeering charges.

Since Sharpton wants to become president of the United States, it is important that we have a complete picture of Sharpton's criminal past, his involvement in fomenting riots that resulted in numerous deaths, and his vicious anti-white and anti-Jewish attitudes. Do we really want a dangerous Jackson wannabe in the White House? Should we elect a man who has built his career upon creating racial hatred while seeking publicity for himself at any cost? The answer is obvious.

Sharpton fancies himself the heir to Jesse Jackson's role as America's biggest scam artist. He has copied his mentor Jackson in a number of ways: Jackson started the Wall Street Project; Sharpton started something called the Madison Avenue Project. For thirty years, Jackson held Saturday morning rallies in Chicago; Sharpton has led them for the past five years in Harlem. In the seventies, Jackson wore a distinctive medallion around his neck, and in the eighties, Sharpton wore a Martin Luther King Jr. medallion in public.

Over the years, Jackson has inserted himself into foreign policy, traveling to numerous countries. Sharpton is now trying to expand into foreign policy with trips to Sudan and to Puerto Rico to protest the Navy using the island of Vieques to test armaments.

Regarding Jackson, Sharpton said, "I still study videos of his old speeches and press conferences. Every morning, while Jesse is on the treadmill watching CNN, I'm on the treadmill watching him!"[8]

Lastly, and most importantly, although both Jackson and Sharpton wear the "Reverend" title, and Al is supposedly a Pentecostal preacher, neither actually pastors a church!

SHARPTON'S PRESIDENTIAL RUN

On January 21, 2003, Al Sharpton declared his interest in running for president in the 2004 contest by filing a statement of candidacy and setting up a presidential committee with the Federal Election Commission in Washington, D.C.

Sharpton's first statement as a candidate was that no other candidate for president "can speak to the disaffected—young people, minorities, women, gays and lesbians—with more credibility and more of a track record of advocacy than I have."[9] This is the same Al Sharpton who once said, "We [blacks] taught philosophy and astrology and mathematics before Socrates *and them Greek homos* ever got around to it" (emphasis added).[10]

The Sharpton exploratory committee was chaired by radical black professors Cornel West of Princeton University and Charles Ogletree of Harvard University.

On April 22, 2003, Sharpton acknowledged that he was a candidate for president after the Federal Elections Commission (FEC) forced his hand. The *Washington Post* reported that FEC officials were on him for not filing a quarterly campaign financial report that the other eight Democratic candidates were required to file. Meanwhile he was raising money without reporting either contributions of $200 or more or expenditures.[11]

Sharpton is apparently planning to recreate on the national stage what he has several times done in New York. For instance, in 1994, Sharpton won 25 percent of the vote when he ran against the late Daniel Patrick Moynihan in the U.S. Senate race. In '97 he ran for mayor, and in the Democratic primary, he nearly forced Manhattan Borough president Ruth Messinger into a runoff, damaging her to the point that when she ran against Mayor Rudy Giuliani, she was easily defeated.

In running for president, Sharpton is again trying to run in the shadow of his mentor, Jesse Jackson. He knows Jackson himself is vulnerable now after his illegitimate baby and other recent misadventures. And like Jackson, Sharpton knows he doesn't have to actually win to "win"—by simply running, Sharpton's profile and clout rise. He is also hoping to gain enough power to force other presidential candidates to bow to him, just as he did in his New York races.

Former New York mayor Ed Koch said, "I don't think he expects to win. I think that if he decides he's actually going to run, it is simply to have a venue—opportunities around the country to speak and become known."[12]

In addition, if Sharpton can qualify on the ballot as a Democrat in twenty states, he could be eligible for up to $16.75 million in federal matching funds.

Jackson ran strong campaigns in 1984 and 1988. In '88, he came in first or second in thirty-one of thirty-six state primaries and gathered seven million votes.

It is mind-blowing that a man with Al Sharpton's well-documented and infamous past would even be considered as president of the United States. This says more about the rampant immorality in the black community than it does about Sharpton. There is no depth to which a man can sink (e.g., Bill Clinton, Jesse Jackson, etc.) that will cause him to be rejected by the black community.

Sharpton still refuses to apologize for past incidents such as the Twana Brawley hoax: "Apologize for what? For believing a young lady?"[13]

When confronted with his ugly past, Sharpton quickly shifts the spotlight to other Democratic contenders. "You talk about me and Brawley—look at what Ted Kennedy had to deal with, and he did very well against an incumbent Democratic president. He's now being lauded by the president of the United States, Mr. Bush," said Sharpton, strongly implying a comparison between his past and Kennedy's Chappaquiddick experience, where a young campaign worker, Mary Jo Kopechne, was killed when Kennedy drove his car off a bridge on the island in 1969. Actually, the Chappaquiddick incident helped ensure that Kennedy would never follow his brother John to the White House.

The Democrats do have reason to fear Sharpton's candidacy, mainly because his presence in the race holds the likelihood that other candidates will be damaged. Conservative columnist Cal Thomas called the Sharpton candidacy "great news for Republicans"[14]; George Will said he is the "Democratic Party's nightmare."[15]

Al Sharpton doesn't care about the Democratic party's nightmare. He is concerned only with his own dreams of power and glory.

FROM DR. KING TO REV. AL

Both Louis Farrakhan and Al Sharpton are enemies of black and white Americans; they are enemies of racial and religious tolerance in America; and they are guilty of fomenting a potential race war. Farrakhan's loyalties are clearly to foreign enemies of the United States, and Sharpton's loyalty appears to be only to himself, to power, and racial unrest.

Al Sharpton is the man waiting in the wings to replace Jesse Jackson as the next great "civil rights" leader. Can you imagine this? In forty years, black America has gone from Dr. King to Rev. Al.

Doesn't that just say it all?

10

Boycotting the NAACP

—⁂—

The NAACP has become little more than
a tool of the racist, elitist Democratic party

During the presidential election of 2000, the National Association for the Advancement of Colored People (NAACP) produced a political TV ad that ran in Texas. The ad portrayed the dragging death of James Byrd, a black man, by three racist murderers. The ad's voice-over featured Mr. Byrd's daughter telling viewers, "My father was killed. He was beaten, chained, and dragged three miles to his death, all because he was black. So when Gov. George Bush refused to support hate-crimes legislation, it was like my father was killed all over again."[1]

This hateful and totally dishonest advertisement was deliberately designed to link the lynching of a black man with George Bush's candidacy for president. This should have been soundly condemned by so-called black leaders, but we never heard a word about it from Jackson, Farrakhan, Sharpton, or the other race hustlers.

Al Gore, of course, did the same thing. In one speech to a black audience, he told them, "When my opponent, Gov. Bush, says he'll appoint strict constructionists to the Supreme Court, I often think of the strictly constructionist meaning that was applied when the Constitution was written—how some people were considered three-fifths of a human being." Pro-Gore leaflets distributed in New Jersey showed Mr. Bush's face superimposed on a Confederate Flag. Gore's black campaign manager, Donna Brazile, told the *Washington Post* that she would never "let the white boys win" (meaning white Republicans—not dishonest liberals like Al Gore.)[2]

During the 2000 presidential campaign, the NAACP ran an aggressive voter registration project under the National Voter Fund. One of the radio ads it ran said, "There are many ways intimidation was, and still is, used to keep African-Americans from voting. Mobs, guns and Jim Crow. Ropes, dogs, lies and hoses."[3]

U.S. New & World Report columnist John Leo described the NAACP's complaints about supposed black voter suppression in Florida and noted that there was a high rate of invalidated votes because of the NAACP's massive voter-registration effort. The 65 percent increase in black voters strained the system, leading to backlog problems and poorly filled-out ballots. Instead of looking at the problems in Florida as evidence of a successful voter registration effort (which it obviously was), the NAACP could only cry racism and voter suppression—just the opposite of the truth.[4]

Since it was formed with the help of Marxist W.E.B. DuBois in the early 20th century, the NAACP has been used willingly as a tool of the Democratic party and the socialists who portray themselves as "progressives" in the Congressional Black Caucus. The NAACP was rooted in a socialist vision, and no change is likely to occur until thinking blacks rise up to reject the racist and extreme leftist leanings of this group.

RADICAL LEADERS LEAD THE WAY

Ben Chavis

In 1993, leftist Rev. Benjamin Chavis was selected to become the new executive director of the NAACP. Chavis wasted no time in converting the NAACP from what had been viewed as a "moderate" civil rights group to an openly radical leftist organization that was going to begin working with Afrocentrists, the Nation of Islam, gang members, and other black racist groups.

To help him accomplish this goal, Chavis immediately hired two long-time haters. One was Don Rojas, former Director of Communications for the People's Revolutionary Government of Grenada under Maurice Bishop. (Bishop was working closely with Fidel Castro to convert Grenada into a socialist nation.) The other was Lewis Myers Jr., a leftist attorney who had worked as a legal adviser to Jesse Jackson and Louis Farrakhan. Myers began organizing coalitions for the NAACP with such groups as the National Conference of Black Lawyers and communist front group National Lawyers Guild.[5]

In addition, according to leftist web magazine *Meanderings,* Chavis held a secret strategy meeting on his efforts to radicalize the NAACP with Kwanzaa creator Ron Karenga, communist Angela Davis, Marxist and Black Nationalist Stokely Carmichael, Rev. Calvin Butts, Harvard professor Cornel West, singer Sister Souljah, and Ossie Davis and Rubie Dee, two black entertainers who have long been associated with communist causes in the U.S.*[6]

Chavis' effort to turn the NAACP into a black nationalist group with ties to Marxists was only partly successful. His legacy lives on in the new leadership, but his role in the NAACP was cut short because of sexual improprieties with a former female aide named Mary Stansel. Stansel had accused Chavis of sexual harassment and discrimination.

---

*Rev. Calvin Butts, pastor of Abyssinian Baptist Church in New York City, is a well-known liberal activist who participated in the Summit on Black Leadership in September 2002 with Nation of Islam racist Louis Farrakhan. Apparently Butts has no problem meeting with Black Nationalists, communists, and anti-American, anti-white Muslims if it serves his own political needs.

When news surfaced that Chavis had secretly paid Stansel $80,000 from NAACP funds as part of a total payout of $332,400, he was fired from his position. Stansel proceeded with a lawsuit against Chavis and he eventually had to pay $245,000 to her.[7]

Chavis landed on his feet, changed his name to Benjamin F. Muhammad, and went to work for Louis Farrakhan's Nation of Islam. In 2000, Muhammad was director of the Nation's Million Family March.

Kweisi Mfume

The NAACP's current president and chief executive officer is Kweisi Mfume, formerly known as Frizzell Gray. As a teenager, Mfume fathered five children by three different women and never married any of them.[8]

Mfume is an example of what's drastically wrong with black men today. Mfume claims that he's provided support for his five illegitimate children, but he never gave them what they needed the most: a loving father in the home.

Mfume's own immoral conduct and his irresponsibility as a father must endear him to Jesse Jackson and other adulterers who portray themselves as the moral voice for blacks in America.

He eventually became a congressman and headed the leftist Congressional Black Caucus before resigning to take over the leadership of the NAACP.

Julian Bond

The NAACP's current chairman, Julian Bond, is a man with a history of association with radical anti-American, anti-white organizations. In the early 1960s, Bond organized the Committee on Appeal for Human Rights, which merged with the Student Non-Violent Coordinating Committee (SNCC). Bond served as SNCC's communications director from 1961 to 1966.

In 1967, the Department of Defense published a detailed background report on SNCC and its ties to black nationalist and communist front groups. At the time this report was written, H. Rap Brown was national chairman of the organization. By 1965, SNCC had renounced nonviolence and its goal of integration and had started agitating against the war in Vietnam.

According to the DOD report on SNCC:

SNCC can no longer be considered a civil rights group. It has become a racist organization with black supremacy ideals and an expressed hatred for whites. It employs violent and militant measures which may be defined as extreme when compared with those of more moderate groups. . . .

The popularity of H. Rap Brown, Stokely Carmichael, and SNCC indicates a changing temper in Negro racist agitation. More and more Negroes are accepting the SNCC policy of violence and destruction of established social order in the U.S. Recent utterances of SNCC leaders call for Negroes to arm themselves in preparation for guerrilla warfare to overthrow the "imperialist" government of the United States. They seek to destroy the present American economic, political, and social systems in a SNCC-defined attempt to gain "freedom" for the Negro.

. . . SNCC promotion of black racism and the advocacy of violence can only serve to increase racial tension throughout the country and possibly harm the struggle for civil rights being conducted by more responsible Negro organizations.[9]

This is the organization that Julian Bond was ideologically committed to in the early 1960s, and his overall political views have apparently not changed to this day.

In November 1965, Bond was elected to the Georgia House of Representatives, but the members of the House voted against seating him because he had signed an SNCC statement describing our war in Vietnam as "aggression" and calling upon American men to dodge the draft. He was eventually seated in the Georgia House, but the struggle turned him into a hero of anti-war leftists and communists.[10]

During the late '60s, Bond traveled to various college campuses and spoke out against the Vietnam War, declaring it "racist." He also spoke in black churches to begin the drumbeat for "reparations" from whites for slavery. In his speeches, he declared that capitalism wasn't the answer for blacks. The answer, he claimed, was a form of community socialism, where each member in a black neighborhood would have a say in who gets how much money and from whom.

As chairman of the NAACP, Julian Bond gave a keynote speech at the 90th annual meeting of the group in February 1999. At this conference, Bond declared that the Republican party was hostile to civil rights and that racism was everywhere. He claimed that the Republicans "have become the running dogs of the wacky radical right" and that Republicans threatened to turn back the clock on civil rights. He noted that today, racism "less often wears a hood and burns a cross. Now it sometimes wears a three-piece suit, but behind that disguise there lurks an evil that our forefathers and mothers fought."[11]

In August 2001, I sent a letter to Julian Bond announcing BOND's inaugural National Boycott of the National Association for the Advancement of Colored People. I pointed out that the NAACP had implied in an advertisement that President George W. Bush was somehow responsible for the dragging death of black man James Byrd in Texas, simply because he had refused to sign a hate-crime law when he was Texas governor. As hate-crime laws necessarily involve controversial issues of First Amendment infringements heaped upon existing and usually effective criminal law, Bush's lack of support for the bill can hardly be called racism.

I also pointed out that at the NAACP's recent convention, Bond had referred to President Bush's judicial nominations as being from the "Taliban wing of American politics" and observed that one of the NAACP's speakers had joked that she was anxious for Senator Strom Thurmond to die. Both comments were over the top.

I then asked, "What is the NAACP doing about our schools, where our kids don't know how to read and write, but they can tell you everything you want to know about a condom? What are you doing about the seventy percent of black babies being born out of wedlock? I believe that your organization has no intent to solve such problems."

In calling for a national boycott of the NAACP, I said that Bond's group had been "reduced, in the minds of many Americans, to little more than a partisan political machine that spends too much time complaining about inconsequential issues [i.e. that there are no black leads on many popular television shows; that states need to remove their Confederate flags; etc.] that have, in our view, nothing to do with actual black progress. Sad indeed."

I never expected to hear from Bond, but was shocked when I got a letter of response, dated September 4, 2001. In it, he responded to my comments on the NAACP's ad involving the dragging death of James Byrd in Texas. He shifted blame away from the NAACP by saying that the NAACP National Voter Fund had sponsored the ad, not the NAACP itself. Did he expect me to believe that, as a leader of the NAACP, he had no control over what the Voter Fund did? In my opinion, Bond lied.

He was honest, however, about his hatred of President Bush and his judicial nominees. He told me, "I believe some of President Bush's nominees do represent an extreme, intolerant slice of American political life—drowning out meaningful debate by fundamentalist rhetoric, a priori proclamations of what society needs—that is easily comparable to the Taliban."[12]

Julian Bond's hatred of Republicans is even more vicious today. On July 8, 2002, the NAACP celebrated its 93rd annual convention. The theme of the convention was "Freedom Under Fire." Bond, of course, was as rabid as usual in his condemnation of Republicans. During his speech, he made it clear where his sympathies lie: "[I]n America's streets, there is gender, there is race, there is religion. Since the [September 11] attacks, people who look like Arabs or Muslims have been harassed, assaulted, even killed."[13]

According to Julian Bond, President Bush is in the snake-oil business and owes his election "more to a dynasty than to democracy." He attacked John Ashcroft as a cross between J. Edgar Hoover and Jerry Falwell. In typical leftist paranoia, Bond declared that "there is a right-wing conspiracy" that is supposedly operating out of the Department of Justice, the White House, and the U.S Commission on Civil Rights. He then accused black conservatives like myself of being "black hustlers and hucksters . . . ventriloquists' dummies" and claimed that white conservatives were able to "buy blacks at a few bucks a head."[14]

This is the man who currently runs the NAACP and claims to speak for blacks. He doesn't speak for me; he speaks only for a delusional group of black socialists and racists who despise America and everything it stands for. The NAACP is not interested in the advancement of "colored people." It is only interested in the advancement of Marxist and Afrocentric policies that will worsen the conditions of blacks and race relations and destroy America.

TAX STATUS OF NAACP QUESTIONED BY CONSERVATIVE BLACKS

Fortunately, many blacks like myself are fed up with the whining that comes from Julian Bond and his leftist friends. It's time that some accountability is demanded of this nonprofit arm of the Democratic party. The game is over. It's time for a reckoning.

In 2001, Phyllis Berry Myers with the Center for New Black Leadership went public with a demand that the NAACP's tax-exempt status be investigated because of its continued partisan activities on behalf of the Democratic party.

According to Myers, "This is a group that, because of its politics, has become far removed from its constituents. It survives through teachers' unions, labor unions . . . . They allow themselves to be the sole subsidiary of the Democratic Party, and it has done a great disservice to black voters. It makes us politically impotent."[15] Myers and other conservative blacks are right to question why the NAACP can operate a multimillion dollar organization with tax-exempt funds when most of its policies and activities directly benefit the Democratic party.

NAACP'S ANTI-BLACK, ANTI-FREEDOM AGENDA

The leaders of the NAACP, because of their socialist and racist worldview, can be expected to come down on the wrong side of nearly every issue that matters to most thinking Americans.

In spite of the policy's abject failure, the NAACP is still in favor of forced busing in order to achieve some sort of mythical balance in public schools between whites and minorities. The fact that busing has actually caused *increased* racial tension between minorities and whites hasn't led the NAACP to change its policies. In fact, it gave the boot to a local NAACP leader in Yonkers, New York, in the mid-1990s, who opposed busing. Kenneth Jenkins explained that demographic shifts in New York had made it difficult to find predominantly white schools to bus black children to. His plea was ignored and he was suspended from leadership.[16]

The same holds true on the issue of school vouchers. Black parents of children in our nation's inner cities would benefit from vouchers because they'd have the freedom to send their kids to higher quality schools. The NAACP opposes vouchers, thus opposing a policy change that would truly benefit poor blacks. In fact, when the local NAACP chapter leader in Colorado Springs, Colorado, expressed support for vouchers, he was kicked out of the group.

In 1999, former NAACP head Willie Breazell wrote an editorial in the Colorado Springs *Gazette-Telegraph* on vouchers. "The poorest kids who need the most help [are] trapped in our very worst schools," he said. For these comments, Breazell was reprimanded by local civil rights leaders and publicly rebuked by Julian Bond. "I was kind of lynched, so to speak," said Breazell after he was forced to resign. Breazell later told the *Wall Street Journal*: "If you join the NAACP, you sacrifice some of your liberties, and if you don't have the group-think mentality, you won't last."[17]

The NAACP has also long been in bed with the gay rights movement. The organization is working closely with the National Gay and Lesbian Task Force to push for pro-gay AIDS training programs in our nation's public schools. Apparently, while it's not okay for black parents to have school vouchers so their children can attend better schools, it's essential to NAACP leaders that black kids learn about sodomy.[18]

Naturally, the NAACP has also been allied with Planned Parenthood and supports unrestricted abortion on demand. It also supports the federal funding of abortions for poor women.

In 1999, the NAACP decided to sue gun manufacturers, claiming that they were responsible for the large number of blacks who are killed or maimed each year in gun-related crimes. The organization lamented the fact that young black males between fifteen and twenty-four are almost five times as likely to be injured by guns as white males in the same age group. Blaming gun manufacturers for the gun-related crimes committed by black hoodlums is absurd and borders on insanity. Yet this is the kind of evil thinking that takes place at the highest levels of the NAACP. These are radical socialists who have little respect for individual responsibility or the Second Amendment and the constitutional right to own guns. Fortunately, sanity has prevailed in this NAACP assault on the right to keep and bear arms. Courts all over the U.S. have rejected lawsuits designed to hold gun manufacturers responsible for the murderous acts of street thugs. A New York State Court of Appeals dismissed the NAACP suit in 2001, and fifteen other similarly frivolous lawsuits have been dismissed in various jurisdictions.[19]

What next? Will NAACP lawyers file wrongful death lawsuits against police departments because they fail to prevent blacks from killing each other? Judging from the kind of irrational leaders running the NAACP, this probably wouldn't seem too far-fetched to them.

The NAACP is totally out of step with most black Americans despite the fact that it continues to have their uncritical support. In 2000, the Joint Center for Political and Economic Studies took a survey of black social concerns. Eight hundred and fifty black Americans were polled and asked to rate their highest to lowest concerns. Health care and black-on-black crime were the highest concerns. Racism and tax reform were at the bottom of the list.[20] Yet, the NAACP still spends most of its time screaming "racism." Accusations of racism, of course, make good fund-raising copy and generate the hatred that radical black leaders need in order to continue filling their bank accounts with donations.

Imagine what would happen if the NAACP and other race-baiting leaders stopped hating whites and actually worked on racial reconciliation? Of course, that's not the real objective of Julian Bond, Jackson,

Farrakhan, Sharpton, or other haters. They have their socialist agendas to pursue, their power and money to acquire. It's tough to get those donations rolling in if there are no racial problems to fix. So, these leaders keep manufacturing new problems or recycling old ones that have already been dealt with.

A recent NAACP fundraising gimmick is to go after the flying of Confederate flags in various southern states. This, of course, helps worsen race relations while simultaneously doing no real good for blacks. It does, however, do wonders for the NAACP's income.

The NAACP is one of black America's worst enemies—much more so than white bigots. By supporting abortion on demand, for example, it has helped slaughter an estimated 13 million black babies since 1973.[21] How does this compare to the numbers of blacks who may have been lynched or dragged to death during the past 150 years? By supporting gay rights, the organization is helping spread AIDS in the black community. More deaths will result from the AIDS epidemic because of their unrighteous stance. NAACP-supported condom distribution programs will actually result in more unintended pregnancies and we'll see more sexually transmitted diseases ravage the black population as these programs encourage the illicit sexual activity that results in these problems.

If the NAACP were truly concerned about black issues, it would focus most of its attention on black-on-black crime, restoring morality to black men, and supporting policies that strengthen black families. It would oppose abortion, support school vouchers (or better yet, oppose any government involvement in education), and support sound economic policy. But as these moves would increase the real-world welfare of blacks and lead toward independence, the NAACP wants nothing to do with them.

IGNORING THE ILLEGAL IMMIGRATION THREAT

While the NAACP runs around crying racism and fighting against Confederate flags and the legal ownership of guns, this leftist black organization ignores one of the most serious problems facing our nation—and blacks in particular. That issue is illegal immigration.

Our nation is being flooded with illegal aliens from Mexico, who are coming across the borders into Texas, California, and Arizona. These aliens are causing crime to skyrocket in these states and are draining our social services. In California, our jails are bursting with them; our hospitals are overburdened by having to care for them; and illegal Mexican immigrants are driving blacks out of their communities. Mexican gangs in prisons are terrorizing other inmates because they outnumber whites, blacks, and other minority groups.

BOND has been fighting against illegal immigration for years in Los Angeles because we can see the harm it brings to the black community and to America. In 1996, for instance, BOND took part in a now-infamous protest rally against illegals called "Americans for America" at the Federal Building in Los Angeles. The protest was organized by Glenn Spencer of Voices of Citizens Together, who was assisted by Barbara Coe of California Coalition for Immigration Reform, among others. The purpose of the protest was to voice support for Proposition 187, a law passed by the voters in 1994 that was designed to slow down illegal immigration in California.

At the protest rally we encountered members of the Progressive Labor party, a radical communist group. Apparently they were there to attempt to intimidate my friend Ezola Foster, who was teaching at Bell High School in Los Angeles, a school with a more than 90 percent Hispanic student body. Ezola had recently appeared on PBS's "NewsHour with Jim Lehrer," arguing that the cost of educating the children of illegal aliens was causing American children to be short-changed. When she returned to school, she was attacked in an open letter written by several of her faculty colleagues who denounced the "contempt she shows for the Bell community."[22]

These communists became violent and started throwing bottles and frozen soda cans at us. The manager of our Home for Boys, Martin Francis, was hit square in the forehead by one of these frozen cans. He bled profusely but refused to leave the scene. Later he had to be treated at a local hospital.

A female reporter for a Los Angeles Spanish-language TV station, K-MEX TV/Univision, Channel 34, had the incredible gall to approach Francis while his forehead was bleeding and ask him if he was a racist! I was standing next to Francis and could not contain myself.

"You're asking that question so that you can use it on your program to make it seem like he's a racist," I told the reporter. "Why don't you ask me if I'm a racist? 'Cause I'm black, right? I love America too, and I think these illegal aliens need to be shipped back to their country. So why is that racist? You're a racist for asking that question. You shouldn't play that kind of game. That's a dumb question. You should be ashamed of yourself."

The violent communists attacked peaceful protestors that day. They even attacked elderly people—it made no difference to them— while the police failed to protect the American citizens, as is too often the case in politically sensitive situations, such as when blacks or Hispanics are involved. More than 150 police in riot gear were eventually called out to restore order.

I also traveled to Washington D.C. that same year to join in a counter-protest against a group of Los Angeles radicals who had organized a pro-illegal immigration march on Washington. At the rally, these leftists demanded free education, health benefits, and full constitutional rights for illegal aliens. I was interviewed by *Human Events* about this march: "They're asking for amnesty, they're asking for free education. . . . Not only are they breaking the law, but they want us to pay to educate them as well," I said.[23]

We're opposing illegal immigration because we know the damage it does to the black community, but the NAACP won't touch this issue. Why? Because they've made peace with the Mexican communists and other leftists who can be counted on to vote Democratic and to support efforts to expand the welfare rolls.

The NAACP doesn't care how much damage illegals may cause to black communities or to national security. The illegal immigration issue should be a top priority of the NAACP, but its silence on this issue is deafening.

TEN REASONS TO BOYCOTT THE NAACP

The NAACP no longer stands for the advancement of black people. Instead, it appears to stand for the advancement of the Democratic party and its partisan platforms. The past two Presidential election races provide plenty of evidence for that. In contrast, at BOND, we are committed to the advancement of blacks and all Americans.

Here are ten reasons why BOND is leading a national boycott of NAACP:

1. *The NAACP Has Sold Out Its Original Intent.* Where the organization once may have sought to give black Americans a helping hand, today the NAACP is defiling its mantle of leadership with petty, partisan, and even racist activities.

Dr. King believed one day we would be judged by the content of our character, not by the color of our skin. The NAACP believes in judging based on the color of one's skin. At BOND, we believe in Dr. King's dream. One of our popular and successful programs is our After School Character Building Program for high school-aged boys. In short, where the NAACP encourages anger and divisiveness, at BOND we encourage forgiveness and unity.

2. *Absent Fathers.* The suicide rate for young black males aged ten to nineteen has increased by 114 percent since 1980.[24] Even when controlling factors such as income, race, and education, fatherless boys have roughly double the odds of ending up in jail. "Each year spent without a father in the home increases the odds of future incarceration by 5 percent, so that a child born to an unwed mother was 2.5 times more likely to end up imprisoned, versus 1.5 times for a boy whose parents split up when he was a teenager," explains Roger Clegg of the Center for Equal Opportunity.[25] Where are black fathers, and where is the NAACP?

The abandonment of black families by fathers is a disgrace and is the number one cause of the unprecedented destruction occurring in the black community. Yet the NAACP appears to be more interested in damaging a Republican president. At BOND, our purpose is "Rebuilding the Family By Rebuilding the Man"—we work daily to help strengthen the family. BOND holds biweekly Men's Meetings, in which the bonds of commitment and family are continually strengthened.

3. *Out-of-Wedlock Births.* Over 70 percent of black babies are born out of wedlock, compared to 26 percent of white babies. Where is the outcry from the NAACP?

In the black community today, out-of-wedlock births are celebrated with baby showers. At BOND we are bringing back shame to this unfortunate practice. Regular Women's Meetings help instill decency in the young women we work with.

4. *Abortion.* Black women are three times more likely than white women to have abortions. There are 1,452 black children aborted every day.[26] What is the NAACP doing about this?

Planned Parenthood founder Margaret Sanger was a racist and eugenicist; she could be called the "Mother of Abortion in America." She viewed sterilization and birth control as a means of weeding out blacks (and other "undesirables") from society.[27] If she were alive today, she'd be thrilled to know that most abortion clinics are located in minority neighborhoods.[28] The NAACP will not stand against the slaughter of unborn black babies, but BOND does, working with pro-life organizations to stop the killing.

5. *Education.* Sixty-three percent of black children read below basic in the fourth grade.[29] Where's the NAACP?

The literacy rate in the black community is abominable, yet there is no NAACP outcry. BOND tutors young people through our BOND Home For Boys, where we house at-risk young men, helping them to overcome anger, enter the job market, learn skills, and start businesses.

6. *Crime.* Murder is the leading cause of death for black men between the age of fifteen and thirty-four, and 90 percent of these murders are committed by other blacks.[30] What is the NAACP's response?

The NAACP will not seriously address the family breakdown and resulting rage which are at the heart of crime. BOND works to find the cause of violence so that it can be prevented. BOND provides individual and family counseling to help diffuse situations before they start, along with conflict-resolution training to solve difficult issues.

7. *Illegal Immigration.* This invasion has exploded in the United States in recent years, pushing blacks out of their neighborhoods, schools, and jobs. The NAACP refuses to take action against this.

This problem will not be solved by politicians and certainly not by the NAACP, and so citizens must do it. BOND has worked with pro-America organizations to help stop illegal immigration, and it will continue to do so until our borders are secure and our laws respected.

8. *Voting Rights for Violent Offenders.* The NAACP is in favor of restoring voting rights to millions of murderers, rapists, and other violent criminals![31]

What about the victims of violent crime who have permanently lost their rights? BOND is not interested in coddling criminals. Instead, it has a prison outreach program to help inmates overcome the emotional and spiritual issues that often drive them to commit crimes.

9. *Dangerous Alliances.* The NAACP consistently aligns itself with political parties and politicians who work against the best interests of the black community.

BOND does not endorse candidates for public office, and allies itself only with men and women of character—which sadly rules out most politicians.

10. *Guns and Blacks*. The NAACP has filed a class-action lawsuit against gun manufacturers, in effect blaming them for black-on-black crime, but statistics show guns don't kill black people, other blacks do.

At BOND, we believe in the God-given right to self-defense, and fully support the Second Amendment to the Constitution, knowing it to be an individual right, and a critical one.

We have asked those who want to help boycott the NAACP to take these actions:

1. Contact the NAACP Headquarters and ask them to explain why they are refusing to deal with the real problems in the black community: 4805 Mt. Hope Drive, Baltimore, Maryland 21215; General, 877-NAACP-98; President's office, 410-580-5600; WashingtonBureau@NAACPNet.org.

2. Withdraw your membership, financial support, and volunteer time from the organization.

3. Spread the word; tell a friend. Call. Email. Let your voice be heard. Do what the NAACP refuses to do—stand for something good!

11

The Father's Role in the Family

—⁂—

The father's importance to the family is primary—
he represents God in the home

The father is to be the head of the family because he has been given this role by God. There is an order that God has established that cannot be violated with impunity. This order is God in Christ, Christ in man, man over woman, and woman over children. The father brings the spiritual identity to the family. Until the early 1960s that role was being filled; then government welfare programs took the father out of the home. Now, mothers are in charge, and this has reversed the God-ordained order. This has brought evil into the black family, with disastrous results.

While in Prattville, Alabama, several years ago, I accepted an invitation to speak at a youth detention center housing approximately fifty-seven young men. The topic of discussion centered around the role of the father in the family.

Hardly any of these youngsters had experienced a relationship with their own fathers, while some spoke only of stepfathers. Their entire life experience had been under the influence of women, who had totally controlled their spirits, minds, and bodies. These young men—inmates and wards of the state—thought like women and acted like women, and not in the ways for which women are praised and loved. They were highly emotional, intensely angry, and very reactive.

They had no respect for manhood. These young men spoke of their fathers with contempt, saying that "men are no good and they are weak" and that there was nothing that a man could teach them that a woman couldn't teach them. Some of these youths commented that when they looked at their surroundings, they could only see weak men, such as drug addicts, unemployed men, and men who were not in charge of their homes.

One of the younger boys told how his father had left him, married a woman who had other children, and had nothing further to do with him. This young boy had no contact, no relationship with his father at all. He felt very hurt about this.

Eventually, most of the fifty-seven boys at this center stood up and admitted their desire and need for a good father and how, deep within them, they longed for their fathers (as we all do). These young men had no inkling of what it is to become a man.

When I see what has happened to the black family and community due to the absence of good fathers, I shudder to think of the destruction to come. And, in all honesty, I believe that if this issue is not dealt with, we will one day have such a state of disorder that it will be totally beyond our capability to control it. When I spoke to those young men, I could see that their need was not for affirmative action, welfare, or more government programs; the crucial need in their lives was the attention of a father. It was heartbreaking to observe some of the boys in this group who stood and shared the need for a close father figure.

On another occasion, I had the opportunity to speak at an affirmative action hearing held at the capitol in Lansing, Michigan. There were representatives from various groups and organizations such as the NAACP. Michigan had been making an attempt to right a wrong by abolishing affirmative action.

Speaker after speaker went to the podium and begged for and lied about the tremendous need for affirmative action. The white feminists, who were only interested in pushing their own agenda, implied that black people are unable to take care of themselves without the special assistance of government programs. That certainly conveys a message to me—that they don't think of blacks as competent people.

Black liberals, of course, are simply selfish deceivers whose first priorities are themselves, not the black race. At this hearing I advised them to get rid of affirmative action because it causes dissension and hatred between races. I also pointed out that the primary beneficiaries of affirmative action have been white females.

I stated that, once again, blacks had been used and that the problem for blacks is not lack of opportunity, not white people, and certainly not racism. The problem stems from the lack of strong families with parents who hold sound, godly principles. Black men need to overcome their paralyzing anger, so they can take back their lives from the enemies who masquerade as friends. They must become heads of their families again and be productive citizens. Then and only then will we begin to see a change in the black family, a change which will extend to the community and to the country at large.

GOVERNMENT'S WAR ON THE BLACK FAMILY

White Americans are afraid to deal "straight up" with this issue for fear of being called racists, but the liberals in government have long waged a war against the black family, especially against black fathers.

It began approximately forty years ago. This attack has not only been sustained, it has intensified up to the present day. Contrary to popular belief, it has not been conducted by drawling Southerners in white hoods. Who is responsible? None other than the programs of the United States government. Its policies are injurious to the black man and his family and are aided and abetted by elite white liberals who hold power in every facet of American life. Of course, black "leaders," be they politicians, preachers, or entertainers, have led blacks down the rathole of racial hatred, blame, and excuse-making, all of which play nicely into the hands of the elite white liberals.

The primary goal of this ongoing, organized attack has been to destroy the man as father and head of the household. These malicious elements have made a mockery of the father by essentially taking him out of the home and placing increasing power into the hands of government. In order to grab control, liberals in the government fed the woman the notion that she did not need a man by giving her special government-sponsored programs; by making the man appear dictatorial, incompetent, and useless; and by convincing her she was her "own woman."

All too often today the black single-parent home is headed by an angry black woman who has been taught to hate men and to view a welfare check as a constitutional right. She has lost all respect for men, and she passes that hatred and disrespect on to her children. With overbearing mothers, these homes often breed boys who grow up hating women—a hatred that causes these sons to view women as mere sex toys that they can abuse, thereby perpetuating the problem.

Many irresponsible black men look at welfare as a free ticket to easy sex sans familial duties. They have no concern for the children they create through casual sex because they figure that the welfare system will take care of their various offspring and multiple sex partners.

In many black homes where the father actually *does* want to be the provider, he is often undermined in his efforts by the black mother who has absorbed the poisonous ideas of white feminists. The father merely represents a paycheck and has little say in how the children are reared or how the home is run.

THE BLACK FAMILY EXPLOITED

Removing the father from the home has opened the door for the black family to be used by every radical leftist organization or so-called leader imaginable, such as the National Organization for Women (which hates men); the American Civil Liberties Union (which hates America); Handgun Control, Inc.; the NAACP; black preachers such as Jesse Jackson, Al Sharpton, and Louis Farrakhan; Congresswoman Maxine Waters; the Democratic party; homosexuals; and Planned Parenthood. They all use blacks as a means of spreading their ideas and destroying American society. Of course, the predominantly America-hating media is happy to be part of all this, giving platforms to and winking approval at these malevolent forces.

Now that the father has been rendered nearly extinct, the black man and woman have no idea how to have a normal man-woman relationship. Seventy percent of black babies are born out of wedlock.[1] Black men comprise nearly 50 percent of our prison population,[2] and the anger of black women toward their incarcerated men renders them functionally incompetent to properly guide their children. As a result, thousands and thousands of children have been taken from their families and are now being raised by the government.

The government, in the form of social workers and judges, who are often liberal, has total control of determining whether a parent is "fit" or not. Because the fathers are not in the home to fight this tyranny, there is typically little the mother can do. A troubled child who ends up in juvenile detention comes under the court's control, and the judge—not the mother—makes the decision whether or not the child will be placed in a foster home. The mother thereby loses all moral and legal control over her child.

Children have been brainwashed by the liberal forces in the government in much the same manner as women. Children, like women before them, have become "liberated" from the need to respect authority in their home. If a mother decides to discipline a child for not taking out the trash, the child can complain and call Social Services. Social Services can then come over and take the child away, even if the child was not mistreated.

I know of many such cases perpetrated by Social Services. In one particular case, a mother called the police after having trouble with her son. The police called Social Services, and they came out to the home. But by the time Social Services arrived, the mother was no longer angry and did not want them to take the child. The agency took the child anyway because they believed the boy's side of the story instead of the mother's. After years of fighting, the mother got the child back, but now she is afraid to discipline him for fear of Social Services. Her son is well aware of how the system operates and, like countless other children, has learned how to manipulate it to his own ends.

In my years working and volunteering in various juvenile justice centers, I have discovered that the experiences these children receive at the hands of the system are far worse than they typically would ever receive at home. These kids are denied their family experience, are drugged with anti-depressants, are raised like cattle with other children whom they don't know, are sexually abused, and often experience horrible mistreatment from social workers (the gatekeepers of these camps), and nothing is being done about it.

The government is creating a generation of lawbreakers with no respect for their parents, America, or God. Many of these children have not seen their mothers or fathers for years; in fact, most of these children have never seen their fathers at all. The gang violence, sex, drugs, homosexuality, divorce, and lawlessness you see in the black community is not due to racism but to governmental takeover, absent fathers, and angry mothers.

BLACK FAMILIES WERE ONCE STRONG

In 1965, Daniel Patrick Moynihan issued a report on the demise of the black family that shocked the nation and resulted in him being scorned for his views. At the time, Moynihan was assistant secretary of labor. The report, "The Negro Family: The Case for National Action," detailed the accelerating destruction of the black family and the social chaos that would result from that destruction.

Moynihan pointed out that a growing number of black men were leaving their wives—either by divorce or abandonment. Husbands were divorced or absent in 22.9 percent of non-white families, compared to 7.9 percent of white families. In addition, while divorce rates for whites and blacks were the same in 1940, the 1964 divorce rate for non-whites was 40 percent higher.

Illegitimacy rates were rising astronomically as well during this time. Moynihan noted that between 1940 and 1960, both white and black illegitimacy rates increased. White illegitimacy increased from 2 percent to 3.07 percent, while black illegitimacy increased from 16.8 percent to 23.6 percent. Between 1940 and 1963, the number of illegitimate children born per 1,000 live births increased by 11 for whites and 68 for non-whites. At the time of Moynihan's report, almost 25 percent of black families were headed by women.[3]

It wasn't always this way. Researchers have found that black families were fairly stable up until the 1940s. As black scholar Thomas Sowell wrote, "Going back a hundred years, when blacks were just one generation out of slavery, we find that census data of that era showed that a slightly higher percentage of black adults had married than white adults. This fact remained true in every census from 1890 to 1940."[4]

THE WELFARE TRAP

So what happened? Lyndon Johnson isn't to be entirely blamed for the demise of the black family in America, but a great deal of the blame can certainly be laid at his feet. The primary tool that has led to the destruction of the black family and the discarding of the black man as its head is a program once called "Aid to Families with Dependent Children" (AFDC). This program was started under Franklin Roosevelt's New Deal to provide aid to widows with children. The program was eventually expanded in later administrations to include unmarried parents with children.

Beginning in 1965, as part of Johnson's so-called War on Poverty, liberals created the food stamp program, which quickly ballooned from 424,000 clients to 2.2 million. This program, added to the AFDC welfare checks, helped create a climate that strongly discouraged black men from remaining in a family structure. It also encouraged single moms to stay on welfare indefinitely.[5]

Here's how it worked: under AFDC, a single mom with a child could get on welfare and actually receive more money if she had more children. She was not required to do anything for this constant flow of income. She couldn't get this free money if she had a man in the house with her. This created a situation where a man who may have wanted to provide for her and his child would be discouraged from doing so if he had a low-paying job. She could earn more money without a man than with one. I have heard many stories about women who have had to lie about having the father of their kids living in the home just so they wouldn't get in trouble with the system or be cut off from aid.

The welfare system also allowed men to impregnate women without guilt or commitment to them or their children. These men knew these woman would be getting their regular welfare checks; with no costs to either sex, it served as an incentive for irresponsibility.

A lady named Mary Hlawatsch called our offices recently after hearing me on a San Diego radio show. She told us of her experience working with black women and families in Harlem in the '60s as a founding member of Harlem Prep School and Street Academy, a project of the Urban League. She had very interesting insights into the tragic outcome of welfare.

Mary noticed that welfare simply robbed women *and* men of their self-esteem and self-worth. She suggested that the welfare system has been worse than slavery for blacks, because work is a spiritual principle; at least during slavery we worked and provided a service, albeit forced. Mary noted that the Bible is so serious about work that it says that if a man does not work he should not eat! But the welfare system has helped gut the black community of our work ethic, thereby crushing our very soul, something slavery could never do.

WHAT HAPPENS WHEN THE FATHER IS GONE?

The black community is not the only community that suffers from fatherlessness. But the sad truth is that more black children are brought up in mother-only homes than children from any other racial or ethnic group.

In 1960, the total number of children in the United States living in fatherless families was less than 10 million, yet today that number is 24 million. Nearly 4 out of 10 children in America do not live in the same home as their fathers.[6]

For nearly 1 million children each year, the pathway to a fatherless family is divorce. Nearly 51 out of every 100 first marriages now end in divorce, compared to 16 out of every 100 first marriages in 1960. No other industrialized nation has a higher divorce rate.[7]

Other factors are at play here as well. In 1960, about 5 percent of all births were out of wedlock. In 1970, that number increased to 10.7 percent, then to 18.4 percent in 1980, 28 percent in 1990, and nearly 33 percent in 1999.[8]

Proving that there are Democrats who "get it," U.S. Senator Evan Bayh has called the increasing prevalence of fatherlessness "one of the greatest social challenges of our time," as he testified before the House Ways and Means Subcommittee on Human Resources in support of a bipartisan House bill addressing the issue of absent fathers.[9]

Bayh pointed out a *Journal of Research in Crime and Delinquency* study which found that the best predictor of violent crime and burglary in a community is not poverty but the number of single-parent households in that community.

Bayh also cited national research revealing that children who live without contact with their fathers are, in comparison to other kids, five times more likely to live in poverty; more likely to bring weapons and drugs into the classroom; twice as likely to commit crime; twice as likely to drop out of school; twice as likely to be abused; more likely to commit suicide; more than twice as likely to abuse alcohol or drugs; and more likely to become pregnant as teenagers.

As I noted earlier, black men need to return to basics if they're going to help restore the black family and save the next generation of black children from violent and unproductive lives. This is an issue of the heart and mind. It must begin with forgiveness, repentance, and a willingness to stop blaming others for the sins of the fathers.

NULL AND NEUTERED

A father is necessary to provide an example of truth, patience, and guidance in the family. He's the provider, ordained to be the spiritual light of the family. Because the father has largely been rendered null and void in the black community, chaos has ensued. Examples of this chaos abound: angry mothers, sex out of wedlock, abortion, suicide, gang violence, low self-esteem, drug and alcohol abuse, government dependency, reliance on leaders to guide one's life, and an abundance of weak men.

The attack on the father is a spiritual attack—a war, as I often say, between good and evil. When the God-ordained family order is broken, a household, and a society, cannot help but have increasing levels of chaos. The government has become the daddy in the black home, and the results have been disastrous.

As a result of not having the father in the home, children feel a sense of emptiness and develop low self-esteem. This void causes children to go out into the world and seek love. As they look for love, they are susceptible to being used in the wrong manner by the wrong people.

The father should be a role model in his family. He should show his children what a good relationship between a man and woman is like; he should teach his children how to work hard, save money, and be moral and responsible individuals. He should teach them to love God and to seek to obey Him in all that they do.

Regrettably, in many cases, the black man is morally corrupt and flees responsibility as both a husband and father. Yet the father is the primary hope for the restoration of the black family in this country. He must return to basic principles and take responsibility for his wife and children. He must treat his wife with respect and display his love for her within the home. The way he treats his wife is the way that his son will treat his future wife. His daughters also learn how a man should treat a woman. The daughter needs to learn how she should be treated by young men she will date by seeing how her father treats her mother.

I remember when I first started dating at age fifteen. I trembled at the thought of disrespecting a girl, *for fear of reprisal from her father*.

That is no longer a consideration for young people. The way that young girls and boys act up today would never happen "back in the day," again, for fear of the fathers. Real men do not put up with young studs taking advantage of their daughters and often charge those that try a few front teeth for the effort.

What role does the woman have in the family? The wife should love her husband and respect him. This doesn't mean she is a doormat or must put up with violence against her or her children. But, absent abuse, she should demonstrate love in her family, modeling it for the children. She has no right to turn them against their father. In a family, she is to be obeyed by her children, and if they refuse to obey, they should be disciplined by the father.

Of course, we are talking about life in a broken society. If there is no father in the home, she must take care of the discipline herself. This requires great patience and wisdom on her part. It is possible for her to discipline if she does it with love and not anger.

What of children? They are to obey their parents and to respect the authority over them within the family. Both the mother and father must be good role models for their children. I can't emphasize this point enough. Words are cheap; actions are what count. There is nothing more destructive to children than to see their parents behaving as hypocrites.

ABSENT MEN IN EDUCATION AND CHURCHES

The black child who lives without a dad in the home often faces the same situation at school. Unfortunately, public education is largely a female-dominated field. The fact is that men have more natural God-given authority than do women, especially when it comes to controlling boys. Because of this, female teachers usually have less control over their classrooms and children tend to run wild.

Male teachers will always have more control over what happens in a classroom—as long as they've not been robbed of their masculinity by feminist-controlled cultural diversity teachings, where real manhood is looked upon as a social defect.

The education of our nation's children is seriously at risk because of the lack of strong male role models in our public schools! Of course, the public school system itself is, for the most part, totally out of control. You'd have to be crazy to send your child to the average public school. You'd have to wake up in the morning and say, "I just hate my kids. What can I do to really punish them? Oh, I'll send them to public school!"

I often speak at public schools, and I can say from first-hand experience that the state of public schools today is just awful, for the most part. Discipline is at an all-time low. I recently spoke at Dorsey High School in Los Angeles, when a friend, Rabbi Nachum Shifren, who teaches Spanish there, invited me. He had been having problems with student discipline. He thought maybe I could get through to them.

Shifren noted that when the school bell would ring, instead of already being in class, students would take their sweet time sauntering in. They also dressed inappropriately; the boys grew ponytails and wore earrings. They also made sexually suggestive comments to the girls regularly, talked throughout the class, roamed around, and were generally out of control. When Shifren attempted to discipline them, they rebelled. According to Shifren, he received no help from the school administration when he complained.

So I came to speak to the class. The topic was "Success." I am a successful person, and I know how to inspire others to success. The first thing I noticed in our interaction was that the boys looked and acted like females. They reacted aggressively when I pointed out their behavior. Only a few would maintain any real dialogue with me. I later heard that, unfortunately, there was little visible positive change in the students. Most continued the same behaviors as before, blatantly disrespecting their teacher, Rabbi Shifren. In fact, I found out that one week later, the classroom was nearly burned down!

We also face problems in black churches where women dominate. Men are largely absent from churches unless they're dragged there by their wives or girlfriends. Mostly emasculated men occupy the pews. Women donate the most money, so preachers cater to the desires of women and are fearful of saying anything that might offend them.

We also must deal with the issue of women in the pulpit. Sorry, but I can find nothing in the Bible that gives any legitimacy to women being preachers and ministers over men and women. In fact, the Bible clearly states that only men should be preachers within a church. One example:

> Let the woman learn in silence with all subjection. But I suffer not a woman to teach, nor to usurp authority over the man, but to be in silence. For Adam was first formed, then Eve. And Adam was not deceived, but the woman being deceived was in the transgression. (1 Timothy 2:11-14)

Again, many feminist-dominated churches have turned God's order on its head by placing women in ministerial positions. This is an evil that must be overturned. If we ever wish to recover any spiritual life within churches, we must insist that only men be preachers.

I have seen, as I'm sure you have, black women preachers such as Juanita Bynum or Taffi Dollar, wife of Creflo Dollar, preaching with apparent great authority. We are seeing more and more of this, particularly in the black community. I've had several woman preachers on my radio show, including Rev. Renita J. Weems, Ph.D., a speaker and author; Rev. Sandra Sorenson of United Church of Christ; and, most interesting of all, Sonia Brown, along with her husband Tom, of Tom Brown Ministries in El Paso, Texas.

All accused me of judging them when I pointed out areas in which they were falling short. They twisted the Bible to have meanings that aren't there, just so they could be comfortable and feel like they were in agreement with it. Amazing what the mind will come up with to justify itself.

We also had Rev. Dr. Suzan Johnson Cook, pastor of Bronx Christian Fellowship Church in New York City, on the program. This woman was very pro-Bill Clinton and in fact was actually appointed by him as a White House Fellow on the Domestic Policy Council. Can you imagine a preacher being in favor of and working for Bill Clinton? Dr. Cook ended up hanging up on me early in the show.

God is not pleased that men have given up the leadership in their homes and in the churches too. This is the devil's plan—to reverse God's order and to create chaos. He's doing a great job of it so far, with the help of weak male church leaders and ambitious women.

The return of men to their proper roles as leaders in the family and in our communities is the only remedy which will cure what ails America. For without order, there is indeed chaos. And without order, families, communities, and nations are destroyed.

12

The Attack on the Man

—⚡—

Men must understand their masculinity

I've seen the soulless looks of young men in juvenile detention centers. I've watched the arrogant and swaggering young black men standing on street corners waiting for their next drug deal or itching for the next gun battle over their turf.

I've also counseled hundreds of men, young and old, who have struggled with what it means to be a man in our morally corrupt culture. Boys who grow up without good fathers to guide them have seldom learned what manhood is or how they should behave in dealing with others. For far too many of them, the law of the jungle is all they know.

One common trait found among young fatherless men is a desire to fill the void of the true masculinity they've never been shown with a false, untutored masculinity. These young men are attracted to strength, as we all are. But they do not see real strength in their world, particularly if they do not have fathers. What they see instead is hypo-critical "good" behavior from phonies or flat-out mean behavior from authority figures. As a result, angry, violent behavior looks like strength to them, and they emulate it.

This attitude is displayed every night on BET and MTV in videos showing gun-toting, drug-smoking inner city blacks. These are their role models, their heroes.

While this false masculinity is a huge problem with inner city black kids (as well as whites who grow up without dads or are influenced by the antisocial attitudes of such rappers as Eminem), there is an even more serious problem for all men: the attempt by radical feminists to destroy any concept of what it means to be a man.

The attack on masculinity and manhood has gone on for genera-tions in this nation, and the damage it has done is incredible. This relentless assault has been waged by a group of radical, man-hating, typically white feminists.

One of the first major open assaults against men was a speech by radical Marxist Kate Millett in 1968. She gave this speech at a women's liberation movement meeting at Cornell University. During her talk, she described the relationship between men and women as being like that of political enemies.[1] Two years later, Millett published her diatribe against men in *Sexual Politics*.[2] This book was eventually dubbed as the *Communist Manifesto* of the women's movement, and Millett was called the Mao Tse-tung of women's liberation. She, of course, relied heavily on Karl Marx and other Marxist writers to describe her hatred of men and of capitalism. (Millett has since spent time in several mental institutions for manic depression and has acknowledged that she is a lesbian.[3] Little wonder she hates men.)

The radical feminists who currently run this movement have not backed off from their major goals. Feminists have attacked manhood at every level of society. They have attacked the military for refusing to put women into combat; fought to bring homosexuals into the mili-tary; demanded that basic training requirements be lowered so that women can qualify by doing less than men; and fought for lowered physical standards for firefighters and for policemen.

Feminists are working to squelch the natural assertiveness of boys and to create "nurturing" and "compassionate" individuals. In short, feminists are attempting to destroy boys and remake them in their image.

Feminists prefer that men be nice, weak, and pliable, like the late Mr. Rogers, or like Bill Clinton, a boy with serious emotional problems who never grew up. Men: don't aim to be "nice," because nice is weak. I'm not telling you to be mean either. A real man is neither nice nor mean. He has a pleasant personality, but do not think of crossing him!

Sadly, many black men have had their masculinity stripped from them by their mothers, coping in that void created by a missing or weak father. Society, culture, liberal governmental policies, "gangsta" rap music, casual sex, and drugs—all of these are just symptoms of the black man's deep-seated problems and corruption.

I have seen far too many young men in my counseling sessions who have been brought up by mean, overbearing mothers or grandmothers. They have been raised in an environment that teaches them to be fearful, shy, and easily intimidated by women. In many cases, they've also been turned against their fathers, who may or may not have been absent from the home. I've also noticed that many of these boys have been smothered by their grandmothers or mothers and have never been taught to think or act on their own. They are absolutely paralyzed with fear and indecision—and this often turns into anger and violence.

Because they've been so oppressed in this way, they develop a hatred for women that damages their ability to form loving relationships in marriage. The cycle of abuse, smothering, and oppression comes full circle, and these young men end up abusing their wives, having affairs, or deserting them altogether.

The young black who has been emasculated by domineering women in his life also becomes a perfect candidate for being seduced into a homosexual lifestyle. Without a firm masculine identity, these young men become feminized and are easy prey for aggressive homosexuals—frequently wealthy white homosexuals—who are looking for sex. These people can easily seduce confused black men who lack money or any prospects for the future.

The young black men I work with at BOND usually come to us angry and undisciplined, and they have a sense of hopelessness that breeds failure. This anger causes a spiritual blindness—a feeling of being separated from God—and it brings with it doubt, worry, and fear.

Of course, the black scam artists like Jesse Jackson and Louis Farrakhan are ready and waiting to blame all of the black man's problems on white racism. This gives young blacks a scapegoat for their failures—and they often turn their anger at their mothers into rage against whites. They've been told this lie so often that they believe it—even when there's no evidence for it.

The real world needs masculine men who are not confused about their manhood or what their role is in society or in the family. The real world needs men who are physically strong, who possess a sound moral compass, and who are unafraid.

Back in the 1950s, TV fathers were shown to be loving, compassionate men, but they were also shown as wise heads of their families. "Father Knows Best," "Ozzie and Harriet," and "Leave It to Beaver" featured solid two-parent families where the father was treated respectfully. These were men who had a good sense of their masculinity, and their leadership qualities were obvious.

The black community had quality family shows like "Good Times" and "The Cosby Show" in the '70s and '80s.

But times have certainly changed. Now fathers are portrayed as idiots, buffoons, or evil. Ozzie Osbourne has replaced Ozzie Nelson. Al Bundy of "Married with Children," a slobbish, sex-hungry man, is a good example of today's TV husband and father. Real men who actually stand for something are portrayed as weaklings and are outgunned by supposedly much smarter females in most sitcoms and in movies.

As a result of this deliberate attack on men and manhood, many men have no idea what it means to exercise real authority within a family. And boys have lost any idea of what it means to be masculine. They have no clue what manhood is about, and there's no one to teach them.

BRING BACK THE HERO

Instead of looking on and laughing while Hollywood emasculates men, creating a nation of whining Hugh Grants, Alan Aldas, and Woody Allens, wouldn't you rather see heroes in the movies? I know real women appreciate real men.

Prior to the 1960s, Hollywood routinely portrayed the hero on the big screen. John Wayne, Gary Cooper, Roy Rogers, and others are good examples. They were men of honor who treated women with respect, but they were also men of action who weren't afraid to challenge evil. They had a high moral code and a sound sense of right and wrong. They knew who they were and what their purpose in life was.

A great example in the black community of an actor-hero is Sidney Poitier. In his roles, he portrayed real masculine strength. He kicked butt and took names—with dignity. Black Americans drew strength, I believe, from his example.

During the '60s, however, Hollywood began introducing the anti-hero into films. These were hardened and worldly men who still pursued the "bad guys" but whose sexual morality was questionable. Clint Eastwood, James Coburn, Sean Connery, and others played these anti-heroes. While they still engaged in heroic acts, they were immoral individuals who routinely slept with one or more willing women during the film.

A perfect example of this in the black community is the "Shaft"/"Superfly" exploitation (or "Blaxploitation," as they were often called) movies.

Today's movie stars are largely obnoxious liberals like Martin Sheen, Alec Baldwin, and Susan Sarandon, who routinely protest against America and our war on terrorism under the guise of being peace lovers.

And many of today's black movie stars are wimps and whiners. I've already mentioned leftist Danny Glover and others. Then there's Denzel Washington, who appeared on "60 Minutes" one time and complained that he was *only* getting $12 million per movie! At the

2002 Academy Awards, Halle Berry became the first black woman to receive the "Best Actress" award. Instead of accepting her award with poise, she got up on stage and went into the most emotional, ridiculous display imaginable to show her "blackness." You would have thought she was Rosa Parks for all the whooping and hollering she was doing about this great breakthrough. (I never thought she could act anyway!) Up until winning her award, Berry was more famous for being charged with leaving the scene of an accident after her car hit another automobile early one morning in West Hollywood. According to reports, deputies believed she ran a red light.[4]

And then there's Whoopi Goldberg, the unfunny "comedienne" and movie actress whom we see all too often either hosting an awards show or making cutting remarks about conservatives. If I never see her again in the movies or on TV, it will be too soon.

Goldberg once said on the late-night TV show "Politically Incorrect," "I'm not sure that communism is necessarily a bad thing." BOND Advisory Board member Dennis Prager, who was on the show with Goldberg, was amazed at her comment. Actually she was just verbalizing what a lot of Hollywood liberals think.[5]

WHAT IS MASCULINITY?

The assault on masculinity by man-hating feminists must be resisted at all costs, but there also must be an effort to teach young black men what it means to be truly masculine.

At BOND, our goal is clear: To rebuild the family by rebuilding the man. Although we deal primarily with men, we work with women as well. Young black men are suffering primarily because they lack fathers who could provide living examples of these manly traits.

What then, is true masculinity? A masculine man is first and foremost one who loves God and loves what is right with all his soul, mind, and strength. If a man is not doing that, he ought to forget about whatever else he's trying to do, because it won't work.

A masculine man is a responsible person and knows the difference between right and wrong. He does what he has to do without being told. He has a sense of self-control and self-discipline, he doesn't take advantage of the weak, he tries to help others, and he's a good role model for young men to emulate. He is strong and honorable.

Jesus Christ is the perfect example of a real man. As we see in the Gospels, his relationship with his father was strong. He had total respect, faith, and love for his father, and so obeyed his instructions. This is what gave Jesus the power he had over evil. Jesus Christ had real love. He was honest, strong, and compassionate. And he could be tough. Just ask the moneychangers in the temple.

On that occasion he displayed a godly, righteous anger—not the unrighteous, judgmental, resentful anger we see so often today. This is a critical point because too often we hear people, particularly Christians, justifying their mean, nasty behavior by saying, "Well, Jesus was angry with the moneychangers in the temple!" As Jesus would say, "Forgive them, Father, for they know not what they do." They do not understand their actions. They are blind.

Please—if you are one of these Christians going off because someone got too close to you on the freeway this morning, or nagging and yelling at your wife and kids—take a breather. This is not the kind of anger Jesus displayed. It is wrong, and you need to stop!

Since the Muslim terrorist attack on our nation on September 11, 2001, our country has seen a resurgence of real manhood. The Mr. Rogers/Bill Clinton "man" has taken a backseat to images of those courageous policemen and firemen who risked their lives to save so many Americans in the collapsing Twin Towers. The softies have given way to images of tough soldiers braving extreme conditions to kill terrorists in places like Afghanistan and Iraq. These heroes hark back to the old days when men were not only courageous but had strong moral compasses that directed them to acts of self-sacrifice and even death for others.

Temple University psychologist Frank Farley says that the hero has returned since 9-11. He has studied culture and the nature of heroes for nearly four decades. He says that a hero is one who exhibits the following characteristics: "courage and strength; kindness, love, and generosity; skill, expertise, and intelligence; honesty; the ability to attract affection and respect from others; adventurousness and the ability to take risks."[6]

CHARACTER COUNTS

We need heroes—and young black men need positive role models they can emulate if they wish to become successful adults. The road to heroism or true manhood isn't found by engaging in hatred or blaming others for one's shortcomings. It's gained when these boys realize that they're going in the wrong direction and that they need to repent, give up their hatred and anger, and learn that being men means loving God with all their hearts and being responsible for their own actions.

Once a boy learns to let go of anger and begins living his life through love and a desire to forgive, his whole demeanor changes and he becomes a different person. The young man who stops hating is on the road to recovery and will no longer engage in self-destructive behaviors that limit his potential. He becomes happy and free to become his true self.

In our After School Character Building Program, we encourage each of these young men to go back to his neighborhood and teach another young man what he has learned. In this way, they're passing along positive teaching to others. At the end of the program, we bring in these graduates and let them tell us what they've learned from our program. This provides accountability for our students, and it helps them learn the concepts because there's no better way to learn than to teach something yourself.

Another powerful factor in our character program is the interaction it fosters between the boys and the male figures in their lives. The boys are encouraged to have their fathers, older brothers, or older male friends attend with them. This brings them together for better communication, mentoring, and even addressing issues that have gone undetected. This, along with the mentoring and interaction of the instructors, makes BOND's After School Character Building Program truly unique and powerful!

Our meetings and workshops also significantly help the critical, necessary process of "Rebuilding the Family By Rebuilding the Man."

13

Why Black Women Are So Mean

—ɱ—

Black men fear black women more
than they do white men

If you go to any post office or bank today and deal with the typical black woman you find there, you'll know why the title of this chapter is so appropriate. I say this partly in jest, but most men—black and white—know exactly what I'm talking about. This is especially true if you happen to live in a large city. Many black women are just plain mean. Why?

The black family has disintegrated over the past forty years for a number of reasons. Black men bear much of the responsibility because of their sexual irresponsibility and laziness, but black women are also at fault. Black men and women victimize each other, and the anger and rage that are produced are passed along to their offspring.

As I've counseled hundreds of kids over the past twelve years, I've noticed a familiar pattern in the wreckage of their lives. Either they are from single-parent homes headed by angry black women, or they've escaped from homes where the father is a drunk or drug addict and the mother has been forced to take over the leadership of the home. When we see an abusive, drunk, drug-addicted, or womanizing husband, in most cases his addictions are indicative of his failure to stand up and be a real man.

Either way, these young black men have no father as a decent role model. They have no way of learning what it means to be a man except through acting out their hatred in gang fights and violence.

In many cases, black women are just as guilty as men in being sexually irresponsible. They allow themselves to be used and abused sexually by men. They give birth to child after child from different fathers and then fall back on the welfare system to pay their bills.

Many of them swing between mean-spiritedness on the one hand and smothering their sons with what they wrongly perceive to be love on the other. The first response comes from bitterness against men—a bitterness that is understandable, though not excusable. As for the other, since mothers cannot provide the kind of masculine guidance that boys need, these moms try to protect their sons to the point that they end up feminizing them. The boys assume the mother's identity, which is frequently that of an insecure, frustrated, and angry person. A boy in this situation ends up resenting his mother because she has smothered him instead of teaching him to be independent and responsible. The father is the one who teaches children to be risk-takers and to be confident and productive in the world. The mother's tendency to coddle actually emotionally cripples these young men.

THE DEADLY DYNAMIC IN THE BLACK FAMILY

There's a deadly dynamic at work here: in a two-parent home, the wife is usually in charge of everything. She corrects the children, handles the finances, and expresses secret (or even open) hatred and disrespect for her husband. Her bitterness turns her children away from their father, and the dad is left with no authority in the home. He's just a paycheck, if that.

Very often, the father doesn't even know that his wife has turned his children against him. He knows his kids are closer to his wife than to him, but he doesn't know why. When conflicts come, he knows he's going to have a big fight on his hands, but he doesn't have any clue about how to exert his authority properly. He'll face fights over finances, discipline, and a whole range of other family issues. All these issues come back to the anger and lack of respect expressed by the woman for the man.

The typical black woman sees the black man as a weakling who can't be trusted to provide for her or to defend her. Her distrust of him has been handed down from generation to generation. Her mother may have distrusted her husband, too.

The man, of course, is not innocent in this. *Far from it*. In fact, as the family's leader, he is *mostly* to blame for the failure in his family.

A black man often neglects the needs of his wife. He neglects her by not standing up to her and by not guiding his family. He does not exert strong and loving leadership in the home.

In February 2003, I interviewed a young black man from Atlanta, Georgia, on my radio program. Our topic was "What's Really Wrong With Black Men." Torey Burse is a graduate of the all-black male Morehouse College and had some great insights into the conflict between black husbands and wives.

Burse grew up in a two-parent working family. His dad was a hard-working man who was honest and paid his bills on time, but he had limited control in his home—especially when it involved his wife's relatives. "I think the way he dealt with it was that he tried to pretend he didn't care and [it] wasn't any big deal. But I could see the look on his face when my mother's relatives would come over and eat up our food, run up the phone bill, and take over the remote control and watch whatever they wanted," said Burse. "They'd feel real comfortable bringing two or three other people over and they'd stay all night." Burse became confused over the lack of control his dad had in the family, but he was powerless to do anything about it.

"Your identity, which comes from the father, gives you your purpose, your goals, your sense of well-being and your sense of family, a place to belong to," said Burse. "And with this support, I can set out on this journey called life. When the father's out of control, the children don't have an identity, so the only people they can relate to are the mother or the grandmother. I think that a boy who grows up in home like this will be physically male but will have the soul of a woman."

> For I the LORD thy God am a jealous God, visiting the iniquity of the fathers upon the children unto the third and fourth generation of them that hate me. (Exodus 20:5)

Burse also noticed that his dad was ruled by his mother as well as by his wife. Torey said that his grandmother (his dad's mother) displayed a thuggish, intimidating kind of attitude and spirit when she wanted her way. His father had never learned to deal with this spirit in his mother, and now he could not deal with this same spirit in his wife.

This is another dangerous dynamic often at work in the black family: the man lets himself be ruled by his mama. This enrages the wife and she finds herself in constant conflict with her mother-in-law. To her, this only confirms that her husband is weak and easily manipulated by the guilt heaped on him by his mother.

OVERCOMING MAMA

If there's to be any hope at all for the black family, the husband must reject his mother's control over his life—and he must be willing to stand up to his wife and take his proper position as head of the family. There can only be one head of a family and this position has been given to the man by God.

Where do black women get their hatred and disrespect toward black men? Well, it often comes from the immoral and violent behavior of the men themselves. But it also comes from the woman's mother or grandmother, from other black women, and from liberal white feminists and lesbians who are waging a wicked war against all men. It also comes from black pastors who cater to women in the church, thereby empowering their judgmental attitudes toward men by letting such attitudes pass without scrutiny.

Many of these pastors teach an ungodly, unbiblical, twisted view of the relationship between husband and wife in a family. They teach that the husband and wife share authority. Women will often say to me when I ask who's in charge of their home that it's "fifty-fifty." If you ever hear a woman say "fifty-fifty," you know she's in charge!

Preachers should be teaching that the man is the head of the family—the president. This isn't teaching men to oppress women. It's teaching husbands and wives to honor the God-created chain of command within the family. There cannot be two co-equal heads of a family. This is a recipe for disaster. Someone has to be in charge, and God has placed the man in that position.

Unfortunately, because of the ongoing conflict between black men and women in the family, domestic violence is at an all-time high. I'm now beginning to see a new trend in my counseling sessions: women are now beginning to batter their husbands instead of the other way around. This has come about as the woman's anger has increased. More and more, women are assuming the positions of men. They are acting like men (an angry woman can never be a man, she can only imitate one), and men are acting more and more like women. Roles are reversing, and these reversals are fundamentally dysfunctional; naturally, women will start beating men.

When women become victims of domestic violence, I often urge them to separate from their husbands until there's been a cooling down period. I then encourage them to seek professional counseling (we provide this service at BOND) from someone who will be willing to deal with the problems of both the man and woman. Both parties are frequently at fault—not just the man.

What's the solution to this dangerous dynamic? First, the man must come back to order—come back to God. He must take his rightful place as the head of the family. He should treat his wife and children with respect but not allow them to usurp his authority. He should exhibit patience, love, and integrity. He must be a good role model for his boys and girls by showing them how a husband and father should act. This display of masculine leadership will help sons become good men, and it will help girls see how a man should treat women. When these daughters are ready to marry, they will seek men who display these character traits.

And what of the wife? She can help restore her disintegrating family by giving up her resentment of her husband, hatred of her father, or disgust with men in general. She must learn to love God sincerely, and then she'll learn how to love her husband the way he should be loved. If he is not lovable, she must learn to love by not hating the man for his weaknesses, and she must stop turning her children away from their father and teach them to love and respect his authority in the home.

THE SINGLE-PARENT DILEMMA

Single mothers face different problems than black women in two-parent homes. They must deal with the reality of having to be mother and disciplinarian. This can frequently have devastating consequences for children.

Unfortunately, the parent-child relationship is injured when a single mom goes to work and must leave her child with a babysitter or in a daycare center. If the child is cared for by a grandparent or close friend, there is a danger that he will bond with the caregiver instead of his mom. In a daycare center, the child is frequently neglected emotionally and learns that the world is a cruel place where violence is sometimes the only weapon that enables survival.

Researchers who have studied the effects of daycare on children have discovered that these environments create horrifying behavioral problems in toddlers. Dr. Brenda Hunter, a researcher who has written about the dangers of daycare to children for more than twenty years, notes that children who spend twenty or more hours per week in daycare are typically more physically and verbally abusive to their parents, less cooperative with all grown-ups, and less tolerant of frustration. Many of these kids become depressed, emotionally deadened, and violent.[1]

The black single mother finds herself in a Catch-22. If she stays at home on welfare, she frequently becomes overbearing and abusive to her children; and if she puts them in daycare, they risk becoming violent and emotionally detached from all human feelings.

Either way, this is a recipe for social disaster on a scale that our nation has never experienced before. The fact of the matter is that God's ideal for families is to have a loving mother *and* father who raise good kids. Moral corruption by both black males and females, however, is violating this natural order. The result is hatred between black men and women, boys who are bred to become prison inmates, and girls who become welfare drones and baby-making machines for lustful and irresponsible black men.

This cycle of sexual sin is not the result of evil "white men." It is the result of rampant sin and immorality within the black community that must stop!

THE WAR BETWEEN BLACK MEN AND WOMEN

God's order for the family is for the man to be the head, for the wife to be his help-mate, and for the father's direction to be carried out through his wife to their children. The single-parent home headed by a woman upsets this divine order. The devastation that results from the violation of this order is evident to all.

The deadly cycle of anger that black women exhibit can often set up their sons and daughters for future failure and lives of violence and welfare dependence. The sad truth is that black women frequently contribute to their own children's downward spiral into welfare dependency and violence by passing on their bitterness to these children.

In his book *Do Black Women Hate Black Men?*, psychologist A.L. Reynolds explains, "Although racism is destructive to black people in America, it falls far short of the destruction caused by the conflict between today's black woman and black man." Reynolds conducted more than three hundred interviews with black men and women and found a disturbing pattern that included the dynamics of separation, hostility, and anguish. Reynolds believes that black men and women must face this threat head on and not blame whites for this crisis.[2]

The *Atlanta Journal-Constitution* conducted a poll of black women and their attitudes toward black men in September 2000. The poll's results were shocking and depressing. Sixty-two percent of the black women polled said that relations between black women and men had worsened in recent years. In 1993, a similar *AJC* poll indicated that 68 percent of black women said that male/female relationships had worsened.

Researchers have found that two out of three black marriages end in divorce, compared to one of every two white marriages. In addition, 44 percent of married black men admit that they've been unfaithful to their wives—double the percentage of whites.[3]

Many black women are simply choosing to remain single instead of risking getting into a relationship that will end in brutality, abandonment, or divorce.

What these women need to realize is what I realized years ago: anger does nothing but destroy the angry person and those around him. Single mothers must decide in their hearts to let go of the bitterness they feel toward the men who abused and abandoned them if they are ever to experience joy and wholeness in their lives.

The Bible warns against allowing our hearts to be consumed by bitterness. Why? Because bitterness not only destroys our own soul and our peace, but it spreads like a cancer to others around us. It infects them with this destructive poison! The book of Hebrews (12:15) warns that "many [will] be defiled" by the "root of bitterness."

Romans 3:14-18 describes the spiritual condition of the person who is consumed by bitterness: "Whose mouth is full of cursing and bitterness: their feet are swift to shed blood: destruction and misery are in their ways: and the way of peace have they not known: there is no fear of God before their eyes."

This sounds like the description of a home headed by an embittered black single mom in the inner city, doesn't it? And what is often the result of this bitterness or lack of fear of God? Those who are embittered are swift to shed innocent blood, and ruin and misery mark their ways. There is no peace in these families, only war and destruction.

In their families, single mothers have the power of life or death, and their hatred or love is what can impact their children for the rest of their lives. The choice is up to the single mother.

BLACK WOMEN IN CRISIS

In July of 2002, the Centers for Disease Control's National Center for Health Statistics released a report entitled "Cohabitation, Marriage, Divorce and Remarriage in the United States." The report showed that black women are facing a crisis in their relationships with black men. According to this study, when compared to all other racial groups, black women are:

- Least likely to marry

- Least likely to marry a long-term cohabiting partner

- Most likely to have their marriages end in separation or divorce

- Most likely to remain separated or divorced

- Least likely to remarry

- Most likely to see their second marriages end

The researchers discovered why almost half of black women's marriages didn't last more than ten years: they had been coerced into premarital sex, had children at the wrong time, married as teens, had family incomes of less than $25,000, and grew up in homes without two parents.[4]

Black women also face the reality that fewer black men are now attending college than are black women. A March 3, 2003, *Newsweek* article described what it calls "The Black Gender Gap" and noted that black women are successfully pursuing higher education while black men are falling behind. The article says that 25 percent of black men go to college while 35 percent of black females do. Young black males also drop out of high school at a higher rate than black females: 17

percent for black men and 13.5 percent for black females. In addition, college-educated black women are earning more than the median for all black working men.[5]

But even more disheartening is the shortage of available black men *period*. Census statistics indicate that for every 100 black women there are only 85 black men—largely due to the fact that so many are incarcerated. *Atlanta Journal-Constitution* reporter Jill Young Miller explains some of the reasons: "A black man between 18 and 24 is eight times more likely to be slain than a white man in the same age group. But the imbalance is even more pronounced when you consider that many black men, while living, are unavailable. More black men—more than a quarter million across the country—are behind bars than in college. . . . Factoring in unemployment and drug addiction, the number of suitable romantic candidates dwindles to about five black men for every 10 black women."[6]

Many black women have become so disillusioned with black men that they're increasingly choosing to marry whites or men in other ethnic groups. Statistics show that between 1980 and 2000, the number of black female/white male marriages tripled from 27,000 to 80,000. At the same time, the number of black male/white female marriages more than doubled from 94,000 to 227,000 by 2000.[7]

As I said before, this isn't a "white man" problem; it's a problem of sin, anger, and immorality that has become normal behavior among blacks. The solution must come from both black men and black women who decide they're fed up with blaming others for their own problems. They need to realize that their immoral behavior is the enemy of the black family and of black prosperity.

14

Save the Children

—⁓—

America's children are the real victims
of a society that has lost its moral anchor

The LORD shall send upon thee cursing, vexation, and rebuke, in all
that thou settest thine hand unto for to do, until thou be destroyed, and
until thou perish quickly; because of the wickedness of thy doings,
whereby thou hast forsaken me.

—DEUT. 28:20.

The soul of the black community is dead—ashes to ashes and dust
to dust. A fire still burns in those very few who have clung to the
values of old, but our days as a people of character, unshakeable spirit,
and respectability are, for all intents and purposes, dead.

I had long been pained by what I perceived to be the gradual decline
of the black community, but it recently dawned on me that the dismal
and prolonged downturn of my people has greatly accelerated. As I

take stock of many of my black brothers and sisters, it is apparent that they are spiritually dead.

This revelation knocked the wind out of me. I had committed myself thirteen years ago to the purpose of helping blacks wake up to see the error of their ways. I thought then that, though blacks had already fallen so far, there was still an opportunity for them to overcome their blind allegiance to liberal leaders. With this new realization, I now sat motionless, wondering if the battle had been lost. Or was there still hope?

After a tumultuous and spiritually troublesome wait in prayer, an answer came to this question. It went as follows:

I saw the death of Jesus Christ, and I saw the death of the black soul. But I also saw the miraculous resurrection of Christ. And with that, I saw a glimmer of hope. The only hope of the black community is for a resurrection of miraculous proportions. Blacks of today must atone for the sins of our fathers. We must repent if there is to be any resurrection of the black soul.

This is a daunting task. Although a sinless Jesus Christ died on the cross and was raised to life again, the black soul died on the gallows of weakness and immorality.

Where is the black community today? The devastation bears repeating. The overwhelming majority of black babies are born out of wedlock, and we are suffering from an epidemic of fatherlessness. The black woman has no respect for the weak black man, and she harbors perpetual hatred for this man who bedded and then abandoned her. The father's absence makes the mother the influential figure to the family, but her anger toward the man who left her is so great that she cannot be a positive influence. The black youth is victimized by his mother's dominant hatred. With no father as a figure of guidance and respect, the child cannot help but yield to antisocial attitudes and criminal behaviors.

The young black man of today is a perfect representation of the overall downfall of the black community. He has no direction, no drive, and no soul. In general, young black men carry with them no sense of responsibility to be productive, no aversion to undisciplined behavior, and no indication that they can overcome the sin into which they're born. Rather than work and strive to move up in the world, they opt to abuse drugs, chase women, and act like immature fools.

Usually when a person is born into dire circumstances, he has a sense of desperation to succeed. He innately feels that he must work hard, harder than all those around him, just to be able to survive. Few of today's young black men feel this drive to succeed. Their focus is on the next marijuana joint. The emasculation of the young black man by the dominant black woman has destroyed this drive for success, and his only motivation now is to lust after women.

Meanwhile, young black girls do as their mothers did, adopting the same vicious, emasculatory techniques. So the cycle continues—repeating from generation to generation.

Obviously, not all members of the black community are like this, but this is, sad to say, an accurate representation of the evil that has taken hold of black America. There seems to be an outright rejection of God by the black community. As a result, I believe God has withdrawn his blessings. When angry blacks spit in God's face, He departs and lets them do what they will.

The penance that the black community is going to have to pay to regain God's favor is incalculable. Ever since the black community in America began forsaking God in the early sixties, all the plagues and curses spoken of in Deuteronomy have come to pass.

BY THE LACK OF OUR CHARACTER

Blacks, in general, seem to care more about welfare checks and material wealth than they care about character, integrity, and personal responsibility. I once had James T. Wilson of the Central Los Angeles NAACP on my television show, and I asked him what was more important, programs or character? He said programs and education were more important than character! Don't believe me? Look at this excerpt from the transcript:

> *Peterson*: Are you embarrassed as a black American that blacks put programs over character?

Wilson: No, not really.

Peterson: Not embarrassed?

Wilson: No, not embarrassed. Because you might feel that it might have been wrong, but you can't feel embarrassed because you have to live with the programs.

Peterson: But you don't have to live with the character?

Wilson: Right. You know . . .

Peterson: (laughs)

Wilson: Character is not a priority.

The man went on to say that programs and education should be the first priority. I then asked, "Bill Clinton is an educated man—when's he going to get his character?!"

I've had this exchange posted on my website for some time. Although it is somewhat amusing, on another level I was quite saddened by his response—not surprised, except perhaps by his honesty. Black leaders have taught blacks to ignore character and to look to welfare checks, reparations, and affirmative action programs as a substitute for character, morality, and decency.

This sinful attitude is being passed down from generation to generation in the black community, and it must stop! Blacks must stop listening to men and women who have seized "leadership" positions and must repent of their immoral attitudes and behaviors. There is no hope whatsoever for blacks if they don't repent and get right with their spouses, children, community, and nation.

This generational sin is evident in the young men who come to live in the BOND Home for Boys. Many display no conscience and no sense of right and wrong. Some of the boys in our program, before coming to our home, saw nothing wrong with smoking dope all day. Many of them have been engaging in sexual activities since their early teens and are habitually inclined toward sex. They think that premarital sex is wrong only if you fail to wear a condom!

These young men's minds have also been poisoned by black racists who have taught them that all of their problems are the result of white racism. And, of course, they're completely lacking in self-discipline. They are used to running wild in the streets and doing whatever they want to do. They're also seriously addicted to TV and to videogames.

These kids are the products of weak or absent fathers, angry mothers, black racism, forty years of failed welfare programs, and sexual immorality within the black community. They're deeply damaged kids, but I have found that most of them can be salvaged if they're encouraged to repent, learn self-control, give up drugs, and learn to rely on God.

Our goal at BOND is to tell these kids the truth about who they are and how they got to be in the condition they're in. Once they begin to see the truth behind the lies they've been fed by black racists like Jesse Jackson, "gangsta rappers," and drug pushers, they begin the long (or short, depending on how humble their hearts are) road to healing.

We teach them how to overcome their anger, take responsibility for their own lives, and stop blaming others for their problems. We also show them that white racism isn't their problem. They are being oppressed by their own lack of character, unforgiveness, laziness, and immorality. Once they grasp these truths, their lives change forever!

Unfortunately, we're just one organization, and there are millions of kids who are falling through the cracks throughout the United States. I have always been hopeful that black churches would step up and help kids become loving, respectful, and productive citizens, but far too many pastors have been reluctant to deal honestly with the root causes of black failure.

One of these root causes is anger, which is really a by-product of judging others. A person holds onto his anger against another individual because it makes him feel better—more righteous—than others. One of our primary goals in dealing with angry young men who come to BOND for help is to get them to let go of their anger and their unforgiveness and judgmental attitude toward others.

RECLAIMING THE FAMILY AND THE BLACK SOUL

I am convinced that the dawn of the civil rights movement was the dawn of unprecedented sin in the black community. This forty-year history of unconstrained sin began with the black man's weakness in letting women take over, thereby violating God's order for the family. By abandoning this God-given role as father and spiritual leader, black men have condemned women and children to lives devoid of spiritual energy and life.

Just a few men stepping up to reclaim their positions as head of the family will not absolve the community of this sin. Many will have to come forward, prepared to sacrifice greatly to rediscover our once-sacred relationship with Him. We know that none of our self-anointed "black leaders" will lift a finger to this end. Their actions push us further downward, all the while boosting their power and wealth. Therefore, we must self-mobilize. We no longer have leaders to rely upon; we have only ourselves. So great is the demoralization in the black community, particularly among young black men, that it will take a great many of us over a long period of time to undo the damage we have done to the black community.

In the film *The Patriot,* Mel Gibson's character says, "I have long feared that my sins would come back to visit me, and the cost is more than I can bear." Well, those sins have come back to visit the black community with a vengeance, and the cost may be more than we can bear. But at least out of respect for the values we once held dear—and the strength we once had as a people—we are still obligated to attempt that ideal, or to die trying.

We must now forget all our petty anger, our weaknesses, and our unfounded rage, and come forward, prepared for the great penance that lies ahead. And we must do so without self-pity. After all, the black soul is dead, and we ourselves are to blame.

MORAL POVERTY

The use and distribution of drugs by gangs is a destructive element that helps create criminals and destroys the black family. I work in the inner city in Los Angeles and have seen this devastation firsthand on the streets and in the faces of the troubled young men I deal with at our Home for Boys.

At the end of 2002, Los Angeles had the unenviable reputation as the murder capital of the United States. By year's end, nearly 600 murders had been committed in the city—most between rival gangs fighting over drug territories. By contrast, New York City, with twice the population of L.A., had only 503 homicides by mid-November of 2002.

The former head of President Bush's faith-based initiative, John DiIulio, wrote a chilling article on the rise of the "Super-Predator" for the *Weekly Standard* in November of 1995. At the time, he related several interviews he had conducted with prisoners in a maximum-security prison in New Jersey, many of these blacks from Newark and Camden. During his conversations with these prisoners, several of them predicted that future gang members would be far more violent and heartless than those of their own generation. One told DiIulio, "I was a bad-ass street gladiator, but these kids are stone-cold predators."[1]

DiIulio describes the typical gang member as suffering from what he calls "moral poverty":

Moral poverty is the poverty of being without loving, capable, responsible adults who teach you right from wrong. It is the poverty of being without parents and other authorities who habituate you to feel joy at others' joy, pain at others' pain, happiness when you do right, remorse when you do wrong. It is the poverty of growing up in the virtual absence of people who teach morality by their own everyday example and who insist that you follow suit.

DiIulio notes that this moral poverty begins very early in homes where there is unmerciful abuse, alcohol and drug abuse, and no love. Unless something is done, says DiIulio, "for as long as their youthful energies hold out, they will do what comes 'naturally': murder, rape, rob, assault, burglarize, deal deadly drugs, and get high."

DiIulio's solution for this problem is exactly what I'm trying to accomplish through BOND: instill moral values in young blacks so they can become responsible family men.

Henry David Thoreau once said, "There are a thousand hacking at the branches of evil to one who is striking at the root." I am striking at the roots of evil in the black community by helping restore the black man to his rightful place as the head of the black family. All of the other problems facing the black community are insignificant compared to the urgent need for black men to come back to God and be good examples for their wives and children.

It is forgiveness—a forsaking of anger and resentment and a willingness to love—that will deliver black youth from useless and violent lives. Yet the scammers reject these solutions because their very existence relies upon the perpetuation of hatred and black racism. These leaders have brought destruction into the black community, not love and reconciliation. Their days are numbered, and what's more, they know it.

15

How Black America
Shall Overcome

—⁊⁊⁊—

A blueprint for true freedom

The devastation wrought on black America by its collective sins is so vast it is hard to comprehend. This book has clearly shown how wicked black leaders have capitalized on this devastation to enrich themselves at the expense of those they claim to assist. It is an outrage beyond words, and we at BOND are working every day to help bring it to an end.

What now? Is there any hope for my people, or are we doomed to oblivion? I believe there is hope, and not only that, there is some good news: according to recently-released U.S. Census Bureau information, despite our nation's recent economic downturn, black families nation-wide are better off now than they were in the mid-1990s. Poverty among blacks—while still twice as high as whites—declined from 26.4 percent in 1996 to 23 percent in 2002. At the same time, black families with incomes of $50,000 or more increased from 21 percent in 1995 to 33 percent in 2001.

More interestingly, some of the increase in family income is related to a growing percentage of black married couples. Today, nearly half of all black families are made up of married couples—up from 46 percent in 1996. While 16 percent of all black families have incomes of $75,000 or more, among married black couples, 27 percent earn at least $75,000 a year.[1]

Of course, you won't find Jesse Jackson, Louis Farrakhan, Al Sharpton, Maxine Waters, Julian Bond, Spike Lee, Danny Glover, or any typical black "leader" heralding the above statistics because they don't fit their lie that blacks are still being held down by a racist white America.

The above statistics are encouraging, but they are only a hint of what we are capable of. So how do we reach our full potential and restore our families and communities once and for all? It's actually not difficult—if our hearts are humble and we are ready for commitment.

1. RESTORE GOD'S ORDER

As I have mentioned earlier, there is an order to life, an order we must return to if we wish to prosper. That order is God in Christ, Christ in man, man over woman, and woman over children. This is not an ego thing. It is not a macho trip. It is simply the way life works best. It creates order and harmony, as opposed to the chaos we've seen in our inner cities. Please don't argue with *me* about this. I didn't invent this order; I just live it! Take your argument to God.

2. COMMIT TO PRAYER

Back when I first realized my life was coming apart, I tried to "get saved" with religion. I read the Bible till I was blue in the face, "named it and claimed it," spoke in tongues (loudly at five in the morning,

driving my apartment neighbors nuts!), and tried to act like a
Christian—but it didn't work. I remember going to the well-known
K.C. (Fred) Price's church, Crenshaw Christian Center, for seven
years—without improving.

One day I asked Price in a pastor's breakfast how I could overcome
and be a man. He just told me to read the Bible and gave no other
words of instruction. I realized that, like so many other black pastors,
he didn't know the answer. The pain of living a wayward life was
becoming too much.

I was ready for change. It was thirteen years ago, and I heard a
Jewish minister on the radio say that if you want to overcome your
problems, shut up, be still, and let God direct your life.

God has commanded us to be still and know Him, to humble ourselves before Him and seek His guidance and direction. I committed
myself to doing this early in the morning and again at nighttime before
I went to bed. My life was changed in a powerful, immediate way. In
fact, I've never been the same since. Simple prayer caused me to truly
see for the first time in my life. I now know the source of my strength,
and I also know that I need prayer to allow me to see my enemies and
overcome them.

I have never looked back and never stopped praying because I know
I am nothing without God's constant guidance. But I have seen many
who will not commit to prayer. Oh, they'll pray for a season, but as
soon as a challenge hits, they'll freak out and forget all about prayer.
Or they'll start staying up too late, getting up too late, and allowing
their minds to be carried away with entertainment. A young man will
get caught up with a woman or make something else too important,
like going out socially or being loved by the world. The inevitable suffering follows, like clockwork.

Beware: do not take prayer for granted. I've also seen many who are
going along fine but end up putting prayer to the side for a while,
thinking they can retrieve it easily whenever it's convenient. They often
begin to think, in the midst of their pride, that the good things that are
happening to them are a result of their own greatness. People like this
are often in for a rude awakening, finding out that they are definitely

not so great when things stop working out for them. Often they end up struggling to get back to the prayer life that was once so good for and to them. Don't be a statistic. When you are ready, commit, and don't look back. Realize that God is the reason for your good fortune, and you'll be ahead of the game.

3. FORGIVE

When I first sat down to be still in prayer, the first thing I saw was that I had hatred in my heart for my parents, and I was sorry about it. After seeing my parents, explaining to them the reason I carried hatred for them, and apologizing, I was free! All my anger, fear, and insecurity were gone and have never returned. Now I am happy and have real courage. I do not feel courageous; I simply do not have fear.

Prayer and the forgiveness it brings are powerful. They cause you to overcome the world. Forgiveness is the key to transforming the black community because unforgiveness is the reason we have been in bondage! The Bible says, "Where there is no vision, the people perish" (Proverbs 29:18). The angry soul is cloudy. It lacks vision. It is truly blinded by anger. Have you ever heard people say, "I got so mad I couldn't see straight"? That is not an exaggeration; it is a fact. They are talking about their spiritual vision. Jesus Christ said, "And why beholdest thou the mote that is in thy brother's eye, but considerest not the beam that is in thine own eye? . . .Thou hypocrite, *first* cast out the beam out of thine own eye; *and then* shalt thou see clearly to cast out the mote out of thy brother's eye" (Matt. 7:3,5, emphasis added). Keep your eyes on yourself and you cannot go wrong. We always fail when we take our eyes off ourselves to judge others.

One problem people have is that when they actually do stop to look at themselves, they see their own weaknesses and end up judging themselves—big mistake! The judgment we cast on ourselves makes it impossible for God to come in and help us to overcome the world.

Forgiveness of others and ourselves is a sign of God's love and allows His love to flow through us. And once we have truly forgiven, we are on our way. It is the same as what the Bible calls being "born again." This is what happened to me thirteen years ago, and it can happen to you if you are willing to forgive.

4. COMMIT TO MARRIAGE

"Gangsta rap" music teaches men that women are whores and sex toys. Women have bought into the same lie and let themselves be sexually exploited, impregnated, and abandoned. The anger that exists between black men and women is real and growing. As long as this anger smolders, there is little hope that blacks can form solid, loving families. The key to restoring the black family is for both black men and women to repent of their anger toward each other and to commit to love.

Black men and women who want families need to commit themselves completely to the institution of marriage. They need to stop sexually exploiting each other. Men must stop preying on women, and women must say "no" to sexual advances. Black men and women must keep from having sex before marriage and must stay faithful in marriage. When they say vows to each other in church, they must commit to love each other and to love and nurture the children they will bring into the world—no matter how hard it may be.

Preachers must make it their goal to promote marriage as the only God-ordained institution that allows for sex between men and women. They must teach that the family is the primary place for children to be loved, nurtured, and trained. The family forms the core of our civilization.

5. JUDGE BY CHARACTER, NOT COLOR

It is critical that black Americans see that the war we are fighting is *spiritual,* not physical. It is not warfare between black and white or male against female. It is good vs. evil! And for too long, too many blacks have been on the side of evil. This must end!

Blacks have been taught lies about the prevalence of white racism for so long that they view every white person with suspicion. Whites have been beaten up by charges of racism for years, and many have examined themselves to see if they really are racists. This self-examination has helped many whites to overcome whatever racist attitudes they may have possessed.

In my experience, white racism is relatively rare. Unfortunately, the black racist leaders must continuously foment racial unrest because that's how they make their living. But black Americans never have been encouraged to examine themselves to see if they're racist toward whites. In fact, blacks have been told by their lying leaders that they can't be racists because whites have all the power in America. And those without power (supposedly blacks) are simply demanding what is rightfully theirs. This is a lie straight out of the pit of hell! Black leaders like Jackson, Farrakhan, and Waters have immense power—and they're the most racist people around! The black person who hates whites because they're white is no different than a white person who hates blacks because they're black. In this sense, there's really no difference between Jesse Jackson and David Duke.

I've also found that many blacks are racist toward members of their own race. Dark-skinned blacks are frequently jealous of those who have lighter skin and complain that light-skinned blacks "think they're better." Many dark-skinned blacks, however, have just the opposite attitude. They feel superior to light-skinned blacks because they look with disdain upon mixed-race blacks and their link to the hated white man.

Black racism against whites takes the focus off real problems facing blacks and wastes energies that should be spent on personal, family, and community development.

6. BECOME INDEPENDENT OF LEADERS

It is wrong to have another man or woman dominate us. Most of us instinctively know this to be true, yet most in the black community apparently feel no shame for having "leaders" dominate them.

Blacks are being destroyed by welfare programs, affirmative action, and the reparations scam. Instead of the self-anointed civil rights leaders encouraging our community to be independent, productive, and moral, they simply continue to yell for more government programs and cry racism whenever they want to shake down corporate America.

Black racists and their condescending white liberal allies have created a welfare system that has destroyed the black man and nearly wiped out black families. Black preachers have by and large turned their backs on the millions of unborn babies killed in their mothers' wombs since the *Roe v. Wade* decision in 1973. They've also refused to condemn homosexuality and sex outside marriage so as not to offend their flocks and hurt their incomes.

Black Americans must reject the policies, ideas, and protests of the problem profiteers. It is time the community realized that these evil men and women are not their friends. They are our worst enemies!

The only leader that men and women should give their hearts, minds, and souls over to is God. And when we follow Him, no man or woman can have power over us. This is true freedom! The day of independent thought must return to black America; it is time to throw off the shackles of the new slave masters!

7. REPUDIATE "BLACK CULTURE"

Much of so-called "black culture"—music, videos, films, etc.—is destructive to the black community and to our future as a nation. "Gangsta rap" music, in particular, is a tool used by violent criminals to promote racial hatred, violence toward women, disrespect for authority, drug abuse, and gang warfare. These are not positive values to be teaching young black men, especially to those who have no fathers.

The message in this type of rap music is a how-to manual for the creation of an ongoing war in our inner cities, and it has the effect of preparing young blacks for a race war, which plays right into the hands of hateful men like Louis Farrakhan. In the cities, gangs are just waiting for an excuse to burn, rob, kill, and loot.

I have had young black men and women tell me that whenever they're in the mood to commit a crime or become violent on the streets, they'll listen to rap music to get them angry. I've also been told that young black men think it's perfectly okay to steal the purse of a white woman because whites supposedly own everything and they deserve payback because of slavery. This is crazy thinking and must be rejected and replaced by a culture of brotherhood and morality.

Similarly, blacks should also reject the term "African-American." We're not "Africans"; we're Americans who happen to be black. Blacks need to get over the habit of romanticizing Africa as their homeland. Most blacks have never been to Africa and never will. For the most part, Africa is a continent of dictators, oppression, bloodshed, famine, and a horrific AIDS epidemic. The African continent is hardly something to be idealized. It represents the very antithesis of what America stands for.

8. EMBRACE WORK AND ENTREPRENEURSHIP

I have been greatly impressed by the lives of Booker T. Washington and the famous scientist George Washington Carver. Both of these men were born into slavery, but they believed in hard work and diligence and became successful men. They didn't whine about white racism or blame any problems in their lives on the legacy of slavery.

Carver, for example, had a horrible life in his early years. His dad was killed in a logging accident shortly after his birth. As a baby, he was kidnapped, along with his mother, by Confederate night riders. He was eventually rescued and raised in a godly home, but his mother had disappeared forever. This man could have wallowed in self-pity and engaged in self-destructive behavior, but he didn't. He eventually became a professor of agriculture at Booker T. Washington's Tuskegee Institute and found three hundred different uses for the previously disregarded peanut, plus discovered all sorts of other products that we use today. He was a success because he refused to feel sorry for himself, he didn't hate the white man, and he worked hard!

Carver and Washington encouraged blacks to get an education and to learn a practical skill that they could use throughout their lives. These men realized laziness would result in failure and a life of poverty.

Black Americans must realize that they live in a cause-and-effect world. They need to understand that if they don't work, or if they get fired because of a bad attitude, they're going to end up in poverty. They need to develop a work ethic and reject the attitude that some jobs are unimportant or beneath them. An undereducated black must commit himself to accepting an entry-level job and working diligently at it. A person who works hard will usually be promoted and eventually prosper. It's called paying dues.

When I was working on the plantation in Alabama, I realized that I needed to work hard if I were to succeed. Back then, black men were embarrassed and felt ashamed if they didn't work hard for their families. Lazy black men were shunned, and mothers didn't want their daughters to date them.

Times have changed due to welfare programs and bad attitudes among many black men. Today, many black women have a better work ethic than black men. These women must handle single parenting and work full-time jobs to care for their children. Black men, on the other hand, are too often looking for government handouts or expecting to be cared for by working women.

I've discussed this with many black business professionals in the Los Angeles area, and the stories they tell me are depressing. They can't find many black men who are willing to work. If they do find them, these men have such rotten attitudes on the job that they eventually get fired. They don't show up on time, and they demand high pay for little or no work.

I know of a black soul food restaurant in the Los Angeles area that primarily employs Hispanic workers—because the black business owner can't find diligent black workers!

Hispanics, Koreans, Cambodians, Vietnamese, and other ethnic minorities in Los Angeles typically have a strong work ethic and want to succeed. In fact, foreign blacks from places like Nigeria and Ethiopia often operate extremely successful businesses in America. I know a barbershop right up the street from my office operated by black Africans, and their business is thriving. But American blacks, by and large, are not succeeding in business. They want handouts and a free ride.

Not only are too many blacks lazy, they're also jealous of others who succeed. This is the "crawdad effect" in action. If you're a fisherman, you've seen this happen. If you have a bucket filled with crawdads, many of them will try to climb out of the bucket to escape being used as bait. The crawdads at the bottom of the bucket will grab the ones trying to escape and pull them back down. That's what blacks often do when other ethnic groups become successful.

One only needs to view videotapes of the Rodney King riots in Los Angeles in 1992 to see the crawdad effect in action. Blacks destroyed scores of Korean-owned businesses in L.A. simply because they were owned by non-blacks.

Blacks with racist attitudes or chips on their shoulders are doomed to failure in the work world. Blacks who think all whites are their enemies are signing their own warrants of arrested development. Their attitudes will be evident for all to see in a business environment, and their ability to get ahead will be severely hampered by such attitudes. This mindset must be rejected in order for blacks to succeed in the work world.

Blacks who follow racist leaders are typically following men and women who favor socialism over capitalism. Socialism has been a universal failure wherever it has been tried because it violates basic economic truths, destroys individual initiative, and saps profits from businesses that could have been used to create new wealth.

Black Americans must learn about and support capitalism. We must learn how the economy operates and how businesses are run. We must reject the defeatist socialist policies that are routinely advocated by the Congressional Black Caucus, the NAACP, and other socialist radicals.

Free enterprise has made our nation the envy of the world. It has given us the highest standard of living anywhere and has resulted in innovations that could not have been accomplished in socialist nations where mindless bureaucrats control economic and creative decisions.

Black Americans who wish to succeed must learn to work within the free enterprise system. If they do, they'll be prosperous. Unfortunately, there's such a hatred of free enterprise among many blacks that there's little emphasis on creating businesses. Those blacks who do try to start businesses in black areas are fearful of having their stores robbed or are afraid of being killed by angry young black men. They're also worried about hiring men and women who often turn out to be lazy or dishonest. As a result, there are too few black businesses in the inner city. This must change!

9. COMMIT TO EDUCATION

Blacks must free themselves from the idea that doing well in school is a "white thing." This is absolute foolishness and results in failure and poverty. Getting a good education and making good grades are definitely not signs that black students have sold out to the white man! Black kids who have adopted this absurd belief are self-destructive and will live far below their real capabilities.

There's another issue at work here too: many teachers are simply incompetent and will not push their students to learn. Many inner city teachers just want to get students into the next grade and out the door—never mind that their diplomas will be basically worthless.

I currently work with a boy who just graduated from high school in Los Angeles. He can't read, but he's trying to learn. Why wasn't he taught to read? He'll be limited in his career possibilities unless he can read and comprehend.

Another boy I work with receives A's in an art class, but he and his fellow students aren't expected to do any work. The teacher is just handing out high grades for students who sit around doing a whole lot of nothing in her class.

I support school vouchers because kids need a chance to get out of schools where the teachers are unwilling to teach. But to me this is only the lesser of two evils. I would prefer that the government get out of the education business altogether. However, the school voucher is a good first step to breaking the monopolistic hold that the National

Education Association and government bureaucrats currently have over students.

I've also seen some great successes with home schooling. As I travel around the country, some of the brightest young people I meet have been home-schooled. The key is a good learning environment that brings out the best in a student and develops a passion for learning.

The sooner blacks reject the notion that education is a white man's value, the sooner we will become successful in life. Getting a good education is not a white thing—it's a human thing, and it's a ticket out of poverty.

10. COMMIT TO TRUE RACIAL RECONCILIATION

Blacks, whites, and other races can get along as long as each race is committed to true racial reconciliation.

Promise Keepers, a Christian organization dedicated to helping men be better fathers and husbands, has been known to encourage white men at their rallies to stand up and apologize to blacks in the crowd for slavery. They have also encouraged whites to apologize to Native Americans for taking their land. While this has been a well-meaning effort to heal the racial divide, it is terribly mistaken.

In the first place, white men attending Promise Keepers rallies are not responsible for slavery. In fact, many of their ancestors may have died in the Civil War to free the slaves. Second, this apology allows blacks to see themselves as victims of white racism, and it lets them off the hook. Are they expected to apologize to whites for their racist thoughts? This places the emphasis on forcing whites to atone for the sins of their ancestors. Expecting more accountability from one race than another—now that's racism!

The path to love between the races is in the hands of blacks and whites. I believe that the overwhelming majority of whites are willing to judge blacks on the basis of their character, not their color. What whites really need to do with blacks is to reject "white fear" and just be honest. Truth is the only way we can be set free. Blacks need to stop assuming that all whites are evil. Assuming qualities about a whole race of people and then judging them for it sounds like racism to me. It's now long past time we let it go.

TELL ME 'BOUT THE GOOD OLD DAYS

It's also time for us to start looking at some ancient wisdom. I used to use a country song by Naomi and Wynonna Judd to open my radio show. It's called "Grandpa (Tell Me 'bout the Good Old Days)." The first verse and chorus go like this:

> *Grandpa, tell me 'bout the good old days*
> *Sometimes it feels like*
> *This world's gone crazy*
> *Grandpa, take me back to yesterday*
> *When the line between right and wrong*
> *Didn't seem so hazy*
>
> *Did lovers really fall in love to stay?*
> *And stand beside each other come what may?*
> *Was a promise really something people kept*
> *Not just something they would say?*
> *Did families really bow their heads to pray?*
> *Did daddies really never go away?*
> *Oh, Grandpa, tell me 'bout the good old days*

It's time to return to the values of the "good old days" when the line between right and wrong wasn't so hazy and when a promise really was something people kept. This song isn't just an idealization of a past that never existed. Anyone old enough to have been a teen in the '40s and '50s *knows* it existed—for blacks as well as whites. Sadly, the sexual, black power, and leftist political revolutions of the 1960s changed all that due to the failure of the father, and we are reaping the terrible consequences in our families and lives.

The return to the proven values of earlier times and to a moral foundation based on love and forgiveness must begin with each of us determining in our own hearts that we wish to make this journey together.

If we're really ready to see any progress in the black community, we must take a long, hard look at ourselves—our anger, unforgiveness, and judgmental attitudes—to make sure we're not part of the problem. Change must start inside each of us. It's not going to be brought about by our attempting to change other people into what we think they should be. We need to *be* that change we're looking for in others, and, of course, offer proper correction as needed. That is real love.

In his letter to the Ephesians, Paul writes, "we wrestle not against flesh and blood, but against principalities, against powers, against the rulers of the darkness of this world, against spiritual wickedness in high places" (6:12). I give talks all across the country, and at the end of my presentation, I like to quote the next verse in Paul's letter: "Wherefore take unto you the whole armour of God, that ye may be able to withstand in the evil day, and having done all, to stand." Only, I like to break it down into today's language, so it comes out more like, "God told us that we need to stand, stand, stand! And when we've done *all* that we can do, *stand some more*!"

This is a call for all of us to tell the truth without fear and to rely on our faith in God to deliver us from evil. We live in dangerous and wicked times, but we must never hold back from doing what we know is right. I, for one, have decided to stand firm and to tell the truth about the exploitation of my community by thoroughly corrupt leaders. I have decided to let Americans, particularly black Americans, know that we do not need leaders—that God is our leader. It is time to claim the true freedom dreamed some forty years ago by Dr. King.

I, too, have a dream today. And I will not stop working toward that day when black Americans and all Americans can truly declare their independence from their so-called leaders and exclaim, "Free at last! Free at last! Thank God Almighty, we are free at last!"

I wish you peace.

Acknowledgments

—⁓—

Iwould like to thank Patrick Rooney, Billy Barton, Francisco Martinez, Ermias Alemayehu, Doug Massey, and Lena Johnson for their tireless effort and commitment to making the unique vision of BOND a reality. Your efforts have never been in vain. Thank you, too, to all the members and friends of the organization. Your support, input, labor, and friendship have truly made the difference and have meant so much to me. I appreciate each and every one of you.

A special thanks to the manager of our BOND Home for Boys, Martin Francis. You have always been there for us and have my undying gratitude.

Notes

—⁓—

Introduction

1. Booker T. Washington, *The Booker T. Washington Papers*, Vol. 1, ed. Louis R. Harlan (Chicago: University of Illinois Press: 1972), 430. One incredible benefit of this 14-volume set is its availability online, complete with a search engine: http://www.historycooperative.org/btw/

2. Booker T. Washington, *The Booker T. Washington Papers*, Vol. 4, ed. Louis R. Harlan (Chicago: University of Illinois Press: 1975), 125.

1. Blacks Need No Leaders

1. Walter Williams, "Riot ideology and 'de-policing,'" WorldNetDaily.com, August 1, 2001.

2. Peter Dizikes, "Mixed Reaction to Jackson," ABCNews.com, January 18, 2001.

3. "Lyons aide tells of inflated numbers," *The Washington Times*, January 29, 1999.

4. Bill Maxwell, "Church can take steps to rebuild trust," *St. Petersburg Times*, December 13, 2000; "Rev. Lyons Replacement Has Record," *United Press International*, December 12, 2000.

5. Sheryl McCarthy, "Church's Motto Could Be: Pastors, Heal Thyselves," *Newsday*, March 2, 1998.

6. Patrick Rooney, "Sympathy for Farrakhan," *Washington Dispatch*, October 21, 2002.

7. Eric Ture Muhammad and Saeed Shabazz, "Wake Up, America!" *Final Call,* October 18, 2002.

8. Jim Burns, "Farrakhan's Comments About US/Iraq Conflict Labeled Outrageous," CNSNews.com, July 9, 2002.

9. "500,000 March in Washington, 200,000 in San Francisco, Hundreds of Thousands More Around the World to Stop the War on Iraq," International ANSWER (internationalanswer.org), January 19, 2003; Sherrie Gossett, "Anti-war leaders charge Nazis rule White House," WorldNetDaily.com. January 18, 2003

10. Nisa Islam Muhammad, "Black clergy to America: war is not the answer, solve problems at home," FinalCall.com, February 20, 2003.

11. Stacey Pamela Patton, "Sin, Sermons and Sexuality; Black Churches Urged to Open Dialogue With Parishioners," *Washington Post,* July 22, 2000, p. B09.

12. "Sex Education, Legal Hookers, Urged at Brothel Restoration Promotion," Associated Press, August 11, 1999.

13. Judith Levine, *Harmful to Minors,* (Minneapolis, MN: University of Minnesota Press, 2002).

14. Booker T. Washington, *The Booker T. Washington Papers*, Vol. 1, ed. Louis R. Harlan (Chicago: University of Illinois Press: 1972), 242.

15. Ibid., 252.

16. Ibid., 252.

17. Ibid., 248.

18. David Greenberg, "W.E.B. Dubois, the writer who traveled backward," *Slate*, April 27, 2001.

19. Joseph Farah, "Congress' Red Army Caucus, Part 2," WorldNetDaily.com, November 23, 1998.

2. The New "Massa"s

1. Clarence Page, "A surprising rise, then demise in black votes," *Chicago Tribune*, November 26, 2000.

2. U.S. Supreme Court Justice Clarence Thomas, "A New Era for Black Leadership," Forerunner.com, n.d.

3. John Perazzo, "How the left trashes black conservatives," FrontPageMagazine.com, July 10, 2002.

4. Ibid.

5. Ibid.

6. Ibid.

7. Ibid.

8. Ibid.

9. Ibid.

10. Richard Dixon, "Traitors Within Our Ranks: Thoughts On How Black Conservatism Contributes To The State Of Racism In This Country," BlackOklahoma.com, n.d.

11. "Rice Blasts Belafonte for Slave Slam," NewsMax.com, October 20, 2002.

12. Ibid.

13. "The CIA and Crack Myth: Media Mendacity," Accuracy in Media Report, October 1996.

14. Daniel Pipes, *Conspiracy* (New York: Free Press, 1997), 3.

15. Martin Hill, "Some blacks believe in AIDS Conspiracy," CNN.com, November 10, 1995.

16. "AIDS: 25% US Blacks Believe HIV Is Man-made Genocide," Foxnews.com, June 5, 1999.

17. Mary Lefkowitz, *Not Out Of Africa: How Afrocentrism Became An Excuse To Teach Myth As History* (New York: Basic Books, 1996).

18. Carol Innerst, "Afrocentrism: Sculpting myth into historical fact?" *The Washington Times*, March 18, 1996; Ralph McGill, "W. E. B. DuBois," *The Atlantic Monthly*, November, 1965, online edition.

19. Keith Richburg, *Out of America: A Black Man Confronts Africa* (New York: Harcourt Brace & Company, 1998) p. xv; Democratic Solicalists of America website lists the DCA as an affiliate of the Socialist International (www.DSAUSA.org)

20. Ibid., 99.

21. Ibid., 138.

22. Neil A. Lewis, "Critical race theorists pessimistic on nation's future: They believe perspectives on events are determined by racial backgrounds," *The Dallas Morning News*, May 25, 1997.

23. Ibid.

24. Ibid.; Heather MacDonald, "Beyond All Reason: The Radical Assault on Truth in American Law," *Commentary*, October 1, 1997.

25. "Williams to speak on myths and realities of Ebonics," Kansas University Public Relations Office, press release, February 7, 1997.

26. Leon Worden, "CCRI foes resort to race-baiting," *The* (Santa Clarita Valley) *Signal*, online edition, September 4, 1996.

27. Michael A. Fletcher, "The Linguist's Fighting Words: John McWhorter Links Low Achievement To Black Culture," *The Washington Post*, January 3, 2001.

28. Paul Mulshine, "Happy Kwanzaa," FrontPageMag.com, December 24, 1999.

29. Ibid.

30. Tony Snow, "The TRUTH About Kwanzaa," *Jewish World Review*, December 31, 1999.

31. Mulshine, "Happy Kwanzaa."

32. J. Lawrence Scholer, "The Story of Kwanzaa," *The Dartmouth Review*, January 15, 2001.

3. *Blacks Are Not Suffering Due to Racism*

1. Lisa Helem, "Poll: Racial split widens. Blacks, whites in U.S. see two Americas," *The Atlanta Constitution*, July 11, 2001.

2. "AIDS Facts," Balm In Gilead (balmingilead.org); figures cited from data provided by the U.S. Centers for Disease Control and Prevention and Harvard AIDS Institute.

3. Kurt London, "The Balm In Gilead: AIDS Advocacy Through The Black Church," *Black Diaspora*, online edition, January 2002.

4. Peggy Lehner, "Abortion and the African-American Community," *Heartlink*, newsletter of Focus on the Family Crisis Pregnancy Ministry, March 2002.

5. Ibid.

6. Walter Williams, "Misdiagnosing Problems Of The Black Family," *Tampa Tribune*, November 20, 2002.

7. Robert Woodson, "When police back off," *The Washington Times*, July 17, 2001.

8. Michelle Malkin, "Reigning queen of the race baiters?" *The Washington Times*, August 21, 2000.
9. BOND Newsletter, January/February 2002.
10. "Interview with Russell Simmons," *The O'Reilly Factor*, December 13, 2002.
11. Bill O'Reilly, "The Rap on Rap," WorldNetDaily.com, August 16, 2001.

4. A Church and Liquor Store on Every Corner

1. Lisa Richardson, "Kwanzaa Fast Focuses on Food Bank," *Los Angeles Times*, January 1, 2002.
2. Ibid.
3. "Black Hall of Fame plans honor for Clinton," CNN.com, October 17, 2002.
4. Elizabeth Brackett, "Race Politics," PBS Online, *NewsHour*, October 16, 1998.

5. Instead of Reparations, How About a Ticket Back to Africa?

1. James W. Ford and James S. Allen, *The Negroes in a Soviet America* (New York: Workers Library Publishers, June 1935).
2. "Audrey Moore," African American Publications (Gale Group Inc., 2001); available online at www.AfricanPubs.com.
3. Timothy B. Tyson, *Radio Free Dixie: Robert F. Williams and the Roots of Black Power* (Chapel Hill: University of North Carolina Press, 1999).
4. Randall Robinson, *The Debt: What America Owes To Blacks* (New York: Plume, 2001), 140, 158.
5. Jim Lobe, "Reparations Lawsuit Seeks Damages for Slavery," IPSNews.net, March 28, 2002.
6. Kevin Beary, "African roots: slavery was widespread on the African continent long before Europeans appeared—and, indeed, is still practiced there." *National Review*, March 10, 1997.
7. Ibid.
8. Ibid.
9. Ibid.
10. Bill Sammon, "African slavery being ignored, group says; U.S. black activists deny Farrakhan factor," *The Washington Times*, March, 15, 1998.
11. Ibid.
12. Thomas Sowell, "Reparations and Irresponsible Demagogues," *Issues & Views*, July 2000.
13. Steve Miller, "Black journalists jeer peer," *The Washington Times*, August 8, 2002.
14. Rev. Jesse Lee Peterson, "Threatening the power of the black elite," WorldNetDaily.com, August 14, 2002.
15. "Hannity & Colmes," Fox News Channel, August 13, 2002.
16. Michael Eric Dyson, "I'm Gonna Get You, Sucka," *Savoy*, November 2002.

6. White Fear

1. Ken Connor, "Senator Lott's Remarks Have Caused Considerable Damage," Family Research Council, Press Release, December 10, 2002.

2. Bob Herbert, "Racism and the G.O.P., *New York Times*, December 12, 2002.

3. John Leo, "A waspish, niggardly slur," *U.S. News & World Report*, February 8, 1999.

4. Ezola Foster, "Running the Liberal Hate Maze," *The New American*, Vol. 16, No. 4, February 14, 2000.

5. Shelby Steele, *The Content of Our Character* (New York: St. Martin's, 1990), p. 88.

6. Shelby Steele, "White Guilt=Black Power," *The Wall Street Journal*, January 8, 2002.

7. Repudiating Jesse Jackson

1. "Toyota Motor Sales U.S.A. Announces Organizational Change," *Automotive Intelligence News*, May 8, 2002.

2. Kenneth R. Timmerman, *Shakedown: Exposing the Real Jesse Jackson* (Washington, DC: Regnery, 2002), 28-30.

3. Ibid. 187.

4. Ibid. 207.

5. Geoff Metcalf, "Unmasking Jesse Jackson," WorldNetDaily.com, March 31, 2002.

6. Carl Limbacher, "First Jackson Biographer Threatened, Needed Bodyguards," Newsmax.com, March 6, 2002.

7. Holman Jenkins, "Business World: Jesse Jackson, Rainmaker," *Wall Street Journal*, January 7, 1998.

8. Patrick J. Reilly, "Jesse Jackson's Empire," *Organization Trends*, Capital Research Center, April 2001.

9. Ibid.

10. Wesley Pruden, "The gathering storm over Jesse Jackson," *The Washington Times*, January 26, 2001.

11. Timmerman, 148.

12. Ibid., 168.

13. Joseph Farah, "Comrade Jesse Jackson," WorldNetDaily.com, March 27, 2001.

14. "Miracle Baby: Jesse Jackson's ex-mistress has no regrets about affair or daughter," ABCNews.com, August 17, 2001.

15. "Jackson Mistress Explodes Over 'Political Stalker' Charge," NewsMax.com, August 18, 2001.

16. Ibid.

17. *The O'Reilly Factor*, Fox News, February 28, 2002.

18. BOND Press Release, January 14, 2003.

19. Marc Morano, "Jesse Jackson's Empire Crumbling, Associates Say," CNSNews.com, January 11, 2002.

20. Ibid.

21. Ibid.

8. Louis Farrakhan, American Hitler

1. David Horowitz, "Myths and stereotypes caused the L.A. riots, and there will be more unless reality takes hold," *Salon*, April 28, 1997.

2. Jan Dodoo, "Nation of Islam," Religious Movements Homepage (University of Virginia); available online at http://religiousmovements.org/nrms/Nofislam.html.

3. Eric Pement, "Louis Farrakhan and the Nation of Islam, Part II," *Cornerstone Magazine*, Vol. 26, Issue 112, 1997, 32-38, 38.

4. Daniel Pipes, "How Elijah Muhammad Won," *Commentary*, June 2000.

5. Ibid.

6. George E. Curry, "Was it conspiracy?" *Minneapolis Star Tribune*, February 1, 1995.

7. "The Biography of Malcom X," CMG World Wide [cgmww.com]; Arthur J. Magida, "Power Play?" *Baltimore Jewish Times*, February 11, 1994. Some sources locate the Audubon Ballroom in Harlem, not Manhattan.

8. "Farrakhan hires one of Malcolm X's assassins," Associated Press, March 25, 1998.

9. Ibid.

10. Cedric Muhammad, "Scripture, The Mother Plane, And Minister Farrakhan's Vision From Tepotzlan, Mexico," BlackElectorate.com, July 23, 2002.

11. Ibid.

12. "Travels with Tyrants: Minister Louis Farrakhan's 1996 Anti-American World Tour," Anti-Defamation League (adl.org), 1996; available online at http://www.adl.org/travels_with_tyrants/travels_with_tyrants.asp.

13. "Farrakhan's behavior is beyond 'shameful' — it's 'trecherous and cowardly,' if not tantamount to treason," Center for Security Policy, Decision Brief, February 15, 1996.

14. Les Kinsolving, "Should Nation of Islam be investigated for terrorism?" WorldNetDaily.com, October 29, 2002.

15. Tim Molloy, "Sniper letter linked to movement," Associated Press, October 26, 2002.

16. Mark Goldblatt, "Hip-hop's grim undertones," *USA Today*, October 29, 2002.

9. Al Sharpton, Riot King

1. Susan Semeleer, "The New Jesse Jackson?" *CBSNews.com*, May 20, 2002.

2. Ellis Henican, "Rev. Al's Got A Brand New Bag," *Newsday*, January 22, 2003 (emphasis added).

3. Jim Sleeper, "*Go and Tell Pharaoh: The Autobiography of the Reverend Al* Sharpton," *The New Republic*, April 22, 1996.

4. Don Feder, "Softness on Sharpton," *The Washington Times*, February 21, 2000.

5. Jeff Jacoby, "The Sharpton Hypocrisy," *Boston Globe,* January 16, 2003.

6. Jeff Jacoby, "The Fires of Hatred in the Age of Farrakhan," *Boston Globe,* December 14, 1995.

7. Greg B. Smith, "Rev. Al's mystery man was a soldier in the mob," *New York Daily News*, July 24, 2002.

8. Jack Newfield, "Rev. Vs. Rev.," *New York Magazine*, January 7, 2002.

9. "Civil rights activist Al Sharpton joins US presidential race," Agence France Press, January 22, 2003.

10. Bob von Sternberg, "Al Sharpton stops in on exploratory presidential tour," *Minneapolis Star Tribune*, May 10, 2002

11. "Sharpton Announces Candidacy," WashingtonPost.com, April 23, 2003.

12. Seth Gitell, "Al Sharpton For President?" The Phoenix.com, February 28, 2003.

13. "Wronged DA Awaits Apology From Sharpton," Associated Press, January 31, 2003.

14. Marc Moreno, "Sharpton Candidacy Would Be 'Great News,'" CNSNews.com, January 30, 2002.
15. George Will, "Sharpton Eyes the Prize," *Jewish World Review*, January 10, 2001.

10. Boycotting the NAACP

1. "Fly Byrd Fly," NAACP National Voter Fund advertisement. This ad began running in 18 markets beginning on September 26, 2000, and was produced by Carol H. Williams Advertising.
2. Walter Williams, "Race Hustling Chorus," *The Washington Times*, December 22, 2000.
3. John Leo, "Racial rhetoric that ignores the facts," *The Washington Times*, December 13, 2000.
4. Ibid.
5. Ron Daniels, "The Rise and Demise of Ben Chavis at the NAACP," *ZMagazine*, n.d.
6. *Meanderings* 1.06, June 11, 1994. *Meanderings* has since been renamed *Gravity*; archives available online at http://www.newsavanna.com
7. Cathy Connors, "Ben Chavis to pay $245G to former NAACP assistant," *New York Amsterdam News*, December 2, 1995.
8. Bill Maxwell, "NAACP leader ushers in bright future for group," *St. Petersburg Times*, July 16, 2000.
9. "Student Non-Violent Coordinating Committee (SNCC)," Department of Defense, U.S. Army Intelligence Command and Federal Bureau of Investigation Counterintelligence Study, 1967; available online at http://www.aavw.org/special_features/govdocs_dod_abstract02_full.html.
10. "The Man Called Julian Bond," *Sacramento Observer*, June 4, 1997.
11. Eddie Evans, "NAACP Head Attacks Republican Leaders In Congress," Reuters, February 20, 1999.
12. Julian Bond, NAACP letter on file, September 4, 2001.
13. Julian Bond, "Freedom Under Fire," War-Times.org, July 8, 2002.
14. Ben Shapiro, "Bond, as in bondage," TownHall.com, July 16, 2002.
15. Steve Miller and Jerry Seper, "NAACP tax status questioned," *The Washington Times*, February 6, 2001.
16. "Busing Updates," *Issues & Views*, Fall/Winter, 1996.
17. "Breazell Is Out," *Issues & Views*, Summer/Fall 1999.
18. Rhonda Smith, "Saying it out loud: Largest-ever survey of black gays ranks HIV as top problem, highlights troubles with white gays, straight blacks," *The Washington Blade*, online edition, March 22, 2002.
19. Martin Kasindorf, "Makers can't be sued for gun misuse, court says," *USA Today*, August 7, 2001.
20. R.D. Davis, "Why NAACP Flunks Republicans (Part III), *The Huntsville Chronicle*, online edition, January 28, 2001.
21. "Abortion Awareness for Black Americans," Solidarity Institute, June 14, 2002.
22. Glenn Spencer, "FAX To Bell High School," AmericanPatrol.com, June 2, 1996.
23. "Immigration Marchers Demand Health Care, Amnesty For Illegals," *Human Events*, October 25, 1996.

24. "Suicide Among Black Youths—United States, 1980-1995," *MMWR Weekly*, Centers for Disease Control, March 20, 1998.
25. Roger Clegg, "1,293,567 Casualties," *National Review Online*, May 1, 2000.
26. Michele Jackson, "A Black Woman's Voice: Abortion Hurts our Community," The Culture of Life Foundation and Institute, n.d.
27. Tanya L. Green, "Margaret Sanger's Eugenic Plan for Black Americans," Concerned Women for America, May 10, 2001.
28. Ibid.
29. "U.S. Secretary of Education Rod Paige, National Urban League and Scholastic Unveil Read & Rise, a Free Guide to Early Literacy," *Business Wire*, July 31, 2001.
30. Walter Williams, "Blaming the Past," *Jewish World Review*, May 19, 1999.
31. "NAACP Reactivates National Prison Project," NAACP Press Release, March 4, 2002.

11. *The Father's Role in the Family*

1. "Out-of-Wedlock Births," *The Washington Times*, January 26, 2003.
2. John McWhorter, "What's Holding Blacks Back?" *City Journal*, Winter 2001.
3. Daniel Patrick Moynihan, "The Negro Family: The Case for National Action," (Washington, DC: Office of Policy Planning and Research, U.S. Department of Labor, 1965), chapter 3; available online at http://www.dol.gov/asp/programs/history/webid-meynihan.htm.
4. Walter E. Williams, "Blaming the Past," *Jewish World Review*, May 19, 1999.
5. Michael Fumento, "Is the Great Society to Blame? If Not, Why Have Problems Worsened Since '60s?" *Investor's Business Daily*, June 19, 1992.
6. Wade F. Horn, Ph.D., and Tom Sylvester, *Father Facts*, 4th ed. (Gaithersburg: National Fatherhood Initiative, 2002); see www.fatherhood.org.
7. Patrick F. Fagan and Robert Rector, "The Effects of Divorce on America," Heritage Foundation, Backgrounder, June 5, 2002.
8. National Center for Health Statistics, *National Vital Statistics Reports*, vol. 48, no. 16, October 18, 2000.
9. Evan Bayh, United States Senator, Indiana, Press Release, October 5, 1999.

12. *The Attack on the Man*

1. Dr. James Dobson, *Bringing Up Boys* (Wheaton: Tyndale, 2002), 162.
2. Kate Millett, *Sexual Politics* (New York: Doubleday, 1970).
3. Leslie Crawford, "Kate Millet, the ambivalent feminist," Salon.com, June 5, 1999, online edition.
4. "Halle Berry charged in car collision," *The Washington Times*, April 2, 2000, C6.
5. *Politically Incorrect*, ABC, July 3, 2001.
6. "Heroes Make a Comeback," *The Washington Times*, October 3, 2001.

13. *Why Black Women Are So Mean*

1. Brenda Hunter, *Home by Choice: Creating Emotional Security in Children* (Portland: Multnomah, 1991), 64.
2. Diane Lorna, "Do Black Women Hate Black Men?" *Call and Post*, July 7, 1994.

3. Jill Young Miller, "AJC Southern Poll: Black Women's Discontent," *Atlanta Journal Constitution*, September 17, 2000.
4. "Black women unlucky in love," *The Washington Times*, October 2, 2002.
5. Ellis Cose, "The Black Gender Gap," *Newsweek*, March 3, 2003.
6. Miller, "AJC Southern Poll."
7. Katti Gray, "Changing Choices/Black women, a group long reluctant to marry outside their race, are now marrying white men at triple the rate they once did." *Newsday*, June 25, 2002.

14. Save the Children

1. John DiIulio, "The Coming Of The Super-Predators," *The Weekly Standard*, November 27, 1995.

15. How Black America Shall Overcome

1. "Census Bureau Releases First Look at African-American Population Since Census 2000," U.S. Census Bureau, April 25, 2003.

About the Author

—m—

R ev. Jesse Lee Peterson is the most outspoken critic of the civil-rights establishment in America today. Often referred to as "the other Jesse" and "the antidote to Jesse Jackson," Rev. Peterson is the creator of the "National Day of Repudiation of Jesse Jackson" event and is also the man behind the boycott of the NAACP, believing the organization to be nothing more than a tool of the "elite, socialist" Democratic party.

Peterson is the founder and president of the national nonprofit organization BOND, the Brotherhood Organization of A New Destiny, whose motto and purpose is "Rebuilding the Family By Rebuilding the

Man" and whose outreach programs include the BOND Home for Boys. Peterson is also the author of the widely acclaimed book, *From Rage to Responsibility*, and host of national radio and TV shows.

An exceptionally charismatic speaker, Jesse is a frequent guest on major networks like Fox, CNN, and MSNBC where he consistently leaves his liberal counterparts in knots. His unflappable, can-do attitude and absolute commitment to truth are the perfect medicine for today's value-challenged society.

WND BOOKS

The pen is indeed mightier than the sword. In an age where swords are being rattled all over the world, a new voice has emerged.

You can find WND Books at your favorite bookstore, or by visiting the Web site www.WorldNetDaily.com.

Center of the Storm
ISBN 0-7852-6443-4

In *Center of the Storm: Practicing Principled Leadership in Times of Crisis,* former Florida Secretary of State Katherine Harris discusses the behind-the-scenes negotiations and backroom bartering that everyone suspected, but no one dared to disclose, during the infamous 2000 presidential election vote recount. Through never-before-revealed anecdotes, she explains twelve essential principles that helped her not just survive but thrive. She clearly illustrates how we, too, can learn these skills that help us in times of crisis.

The Savage Nation
ISBN 0-7852-6353-5

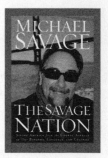

The Savage Nation: Saving America from the Liberal Assault on our Borders, Language, and Culture warns that our country is losing its identity and becoming a victim of political correctness, unmonitored immigration, and socialistic ideals. Michael Savage, whose program is the fourth largest radio talk show and is heard on more than three hundred stations coast to coast, uses bold, biting, and hilarious straight talk to take aim at the sacred cows of our ever-eroding culture and wages war against the "group of psychopaths" known as PETA, the ACLU, and the liberal media.

Taking America Back
ISBN 0-7852-6392-6

"Joseph Farah has written a thought-provoking recipe for reclaiming America's heritage of liberty and self-governance. I don't agree with all the solutions proposed here, but Farah definitely nails the problems."

—**Rush Limbaugh**
Host of America's #1 Talk Program,
The Rush Limbaugh Show

"I don't agree with everything Joseph Farah says in *Taking America Back,* but he has written a provocative, from-the-heart call to action. It's a must-read for anyone who wonders how we can expand liberty and reclaim the vision of our founders."

—**Sean Hannity**
Author of *Let Freedom Ring* and Cohost of *Hannity and Colmes* on FOX News

"Joseph Farah and I share a fierce passion for protecting children and a belief that without the Ten Commandments there would be no U.S. Constitution or Bill of Rights. Every American who shares our convictions should read this book."

—**Dr. Laura C. Schlessinger**
Author of *The Ten Commandments*

First Strike
ISBN 0-7852-6354-3

September 11, 2001, did not represent the first aerial assault against the American mainland. The first came on July 17, 1996, with the downing of TWA Flight 800. First Strike looks in detail at what people saw and heard on that fateful night. With an impressive array of facts, Jack Cashill and James Sanders show the relationship between events in July 1996 and September 2001 and proclaim how and why the American government has attempted to cover up the truth.

Seen and Heard
ISBN 0-7852-6368-3

You've heard the saying "Children should be seen and not heard." But teen political writer Kyle Williams is challenging that adage and making a name for himself in the process. As the youngest columnist for WorldNetDaily.com, he has tackled subjects such as abortion, homosexual rights, separation of church and state, and the public school system. In *Seen and Heard*, Williams again takes on the establishment, offering clear evidence that a leftist agenda is at work in our nation. His lively, energetic analysis of current events will leave readers with an understanding of the attack on traditional family values that is taking place daily. Williams's writing style—sound logic infused with passion and conviction—makes *Seen and Heard* both informative and entertaining.

Crude Politics
ISBN 0-7852-6271-7

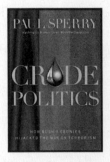

In *Crude Politics*, WorldNetDaily.com's Washington bureau chief Paul Sperry presents alarming evidence that the Bush administration diplomats resumed talks with Pakistani officials over a gas and oil pipeline in Afghanistan while the United States was still reeling from the horror of September 11, 2001. Paul Sperry contends that, true to America's foreign policy of the last century, the Bush administration seized the opportunity to use the attacks as reason to oust the Taliban—the major obstacle blocking plans for the pipeline.

Journalistic Fraud
0-7852-6104-4

For over a hundred years, the *New York Times* has purported to present straight news and hard facts. But, as Bob Kohn shows in *Journalistic Fraud*, the founders' original vision has been hijacked, and today, instead of straight news, readers are given mere editorial under the pretense of objective journalism. Kohn, a lifelong reader of the *Times*, shows point by point the methods by which the *Times'* mission has been subverted by the present management and how such fraudulence directly corrupts hundreds of news agencies across the world.

Breach of Trust
0-7852-6220-2

Breach of Trust is Tom Coburn's gripping story of how he and other Republican revolutionaries took Congress by storm as part of the historic Class of '94, tried to wrest control from the hands of career politicians and push forward with legislation that would dramatically limit the size and scope of government, but found that Washington was unwilling to change. With candor and integrity and one of the most original voices in politics today, Coburn takes you directly into his closed-door conversations with policymakers and sheds new light on the rampant misuse of government funds, shameless attempts to "buy" votes, and the unbelievable ways the system often turns politicians against their own constituents. He also reaffirms and demands every voter's privilege to reclaim America and return to the founder's intent of a government by the people and for the people.

Pick it up at your favorite bookstore
or through <u>www.WorldNetDaily.com</u>.

Available November 2003 from WND Books

Triangle of Death
0-7852-6153-2

A Kennedy assassination book like no other, *Triangle of Death* lies the blame for JFK's murder at the feet of the CIA controlled government of South Vietnam, the French global heroin syndicate, and the New Orleans Mafia. Using KGB documents, a new interview with one of the primary players, and federal documents that have only recently been declassified or released *exclusively* to the authors, O'Leary and Seymour have painstakingly researched and scrupulously corroborated every last detail, combining the popular notions of other theorists with little-known and often-overlooked facts to build a monumental case that is both shocking and convincing. It will change everything you believed—or didn't believe—about the suspicious death of JFK.

Uncle Sam's Plantation
0-7852-6219-9

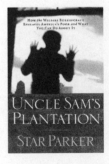

Uncle Sam's Plantation is an incisive look at how government manipulates, controls, and ultimately devastates the lives of the poor—and what we as Americans must do to stop it. Argued with the fresh perspective, hard-won intelligence, and fierce yet compassionate heart of a woman who has been chewed up and spit out by our country's ruthless welfare system, this book sheds much-needed light on the bungled bureaucratic attempts to end poverty and reveals the insidious deceptions perpetrated by self-serving politicians. It's a freedom call for every American to shed the shackles of government handouts and journey toward a future of equality and prosperity for all.

Rev. Jesse Lee Peterson is the Founder and President of **BOND**, the Brotherhood Organization of A New Destiny, whose purpose is "Rebuilding the Family By Rebuilding the Man." Since 1990, BOND has been helping men and their families—particularly in major urban areas—overcome life's challenges, and reaffirm their commitment to God, family, community, and country. The commitment of the organization stresses the importance of self-reliance and strong character.

BOND holds regularly-scheduled meetings and Sunday Services, has entrepreneur, mentor, and After School Character Building Programs, operates the BOND Home for Boys, hosts ongoing workshops and seminars, and offers individual/ family counseling. BOND provides speakers for organizations, events, churches, etc. We publicize our message through our Newsletter, website (www.bondinfo.org), radio, and television.

BOND is headquartered in Los Angeles, California. Membership is $100 per year, and includes a one-year BOND Newsletter Subscription (6 issues — a $35 value), plus 10% off any BOND materials or activities. Your support is absolutely indispensable to our success. BOND is a 501 (C) (3) organization, and contributions are tax-deductible to the amount allowable by law.

• Yes, I want to help Rev. Peterson and his organization, BOND, take on the Scammers and help turn America around! I would like to:

❏ Become a BOND Member ($100, includes Newsletter Subscription — a $35 value)

❏ Make a donation of:

    ❏ $25 ❏ $50 ❏ $100 ❏ $500 ❏ $1,000 ❏ Other $_____

❏ Subscribe to the BOND Newsletter ($35)

❏ My check, payable to "BOND", is enclosed

❏ Please charge $_____ to: (circle one) Mastercard • Visa

    Card # _____-_____-_____-_____

    Expires_____ / _____   Daytime phone (____) _____
           MO   YR

    Cardholder's Signature_____

You can also make a donation via MasterCard / Visa, by calling 1-800-411-BOND (2663). To donate with your credit card online, go to our secure website at www.bondinfo.org. Mailing address: BOND, P.O. Box 35090, Los Angeles, CA 90035-0090.

Thank you for your support!